BURLINGTON ZEPHYRS

GERRY SOUTER

specialtypress
PUBLISHERS AND WHOLESALERS

Published by
Specialty Press Publishers and Wholesalers
39966 Grand Avenue
North Branch, MN 55056
(800) 895-4585 or (651) 277-1400
http://www.specialtypress.com

ISBN 978-1-58007-191-8
SP082P

Material contained in this book is intended for historical and entertainment value only, and is not to be construed as usable for train or component restoration, maintenance, or use.

Printed in USA

Front Cover: *Still gleaming in the morning sun, the stainless-steel Pioneer Zephyr steams at a station platform in 1960, the year of its retirement. Railroads were loading up with diesel locomotives as fast as they could scrap their old steamers and it was this three-car wonder that showed the way. (Jim Neubauer Collection)*

Title Page: *Even in retirement, the 9908 Silver Charger projects a massive arrogance that made heads turn in its prime. The volunteers at the Museum of Transportation still climb inside every few months, crank over the big 567 diesel engine, and let it idle for a while. Without too much work, they claim the 9908 could shoulder its way back out onto the main. (Gerry Souter Photo)*

Back Cover, Upper Left: *Looking from the rear of the power car, the Winton engine and its annealed steel bed virtually fill the engine compartment – and this is with major components still on the shop floor getting individual attention. The two cooling fans above the engineer's cab are clearly seen, but many lube oil and water tanks as well as the electrical cabinet are missing, as is the floor on either side of the engine bed. (Gerry Souter Photo)*

Back Cover, Upper Right: *Winton 600-hp diesel engine sits on two skids on the shop floor with its eight pistons drawn out for reconditioning. The color of the piston chambers indicates there is a lot of work ahead. (Courtesy, Flying Yankee Restoration Group)*

Back Cover, Lower Right: *Running at the same time as the 9908 Silver Charger, the 2-10-0 steamer graphically demonstrates the jump in aerodynamic technology between the steam era and the streamlined diesel era ushered in by the Burlington Zephyrs. Every steam locomotive ever built had the same basic components as the earliest steamers built back in the 1820s – only updated and made more efficient. The Zephyrs were new technology from the wheels up. (Gerry Souter Photo)*

TABLE OF CONTENTS

DEDICATION

To Dave Newsted, for long conversations sorely missed.

PROLOGUE

When a class of trains grows from a legend, that class has a lot to live up to, and that's exactly what happened to the Burlington Zephyrs. There was nothing like them then and there has been nothing like them since. Yet the day of the Zephyr's big debut seemed almost anticlimactic. People lined the trackside from Denver to Chicago to witness the record run. All the switches on the main were spiked open. Every road that crossed the tracks had a Burlington employee on duty with a flag to stop cars. There were even some folks who skipped the soup line that afternoon in 1934 to watch the first Zephyr streamliner go by.

Some of them remembered the day in May 1893 when the New York Central & Hudson River Express, numbered 999, a high-stepping steamer, exploded down a measured mile in 32 seconds with old Charley Hogan at the throttle. The ground shook, side rods blurred, the firebox glowed cherry red, and that iron monster hammered the high iron on 86-inch drivers, sucking ash and dust behind her in a swirling maelstrom – there and gone at 112 mph.

Now, here came the Zephyr, No. 9900, the silver streak, the record-breaker, and everybody watched the tracks that wrapped around the hillside and listened for the engine's roar and the crash of steel on steel. There she was, gleaming in the sun, low to the track as if she was fastened to the rails rather than riding on them. Her diesel engine made a motorcycle-like rumble sound, the chatter of pistons, but deeper, as she glided with no big show or fuss. She swept on by – all fluted steel and rounded corners and whirring wheels. Like the old 999, she was there and gone, but the fillings were still in your teeth. She was modern and slippery in the air, not punching a hole in the breeze, but slicing through it like a hot knife.

Everybody on the hillside wanted to ride on that slippery silver train because that was the future.

INTRODUCTION

The first Burlington Zephyr rolled out onto the rails at the Edward G. Budd Manufacturing Plant in Philadelphia on April 7, 1934. There wasn't a piece of her that didn't gleam. The next thing that caught the observer's eye was her length. She only stretched out to 197 feet, enough to seat and feed 72 passengers, with room for their bags and space to spare for the US Mail. With the power car up front and two coaches behind, she only weighed about 100 tons. One stan-

dard heavyweight passenger car weighed almost that much.

A 600-gallon load of diesel fuel drove her 1,000 miles, non-stop if necessary. The Zephyr didn't ride high above the rails – she was built low to the ground and hunkered down on only 16 wheels for all three units. That meant she ran on 20 fewer wheels than three standard passenger cars and that added up to less friction on steel when she throttled up to over 100 mph. That's what No. 9900 was all about:

speed, efficiency, and high style, exactly what it took to revive America's railroad passenger service in the middle of the Great Depression.

The Zephyrs were truly legends of their eras. Each succeeding generation reflected the latest technological changes and improvements and each served out its assigned duties with distinction. This book looks at the challenges the Zephyrs faced and the technologies employed to advance this marvel in rail transportation.

ACKNOWLEDGMENTS

A book like this requires help from a number of experts on the subject: archivists, collectors, rail fans, historians, hobbyists, and authors. A technical examination of the Burlington Zephyrs and the B&M *Flying Yankee* as representatives of a revolutionary design concept from the Budd Manufacturing Company and the Electro-Motive Corporation requires more than looking at bits and pieces on the shop floor. These very first diesel streamliners changed the history of railroads throughout the world. To fully understand that fact requires the accumulated vision of a lot of people from various viewpoints.

Dave Lotz of the Burlington Route Historical Society generously opened his own collection and that of the Society to us and pointed the way to ardent rail historians such as Jim Singer and superb photographer Jim Neubauer. The Society's *Burlington Bulletin* No. 13 from 1984 provided a springboard for our research with its excellent and exhaustive text written by Hol Wagner and pages of credited illustrations. Clint Chamberlin at North East Rails (www.northeast.railfan.net/home.html) put us in contact with Jim Kerr and his pre-Zephyr photos of early Budd diesel-electric car designs.

The Burlington Northern Santa Fe Archive licensed us photos available nowhere else through accommodating archivist Richard Russack. Lindsey MacAllister dug out dusty three-ring binders of slides taken during the last resurrection of the *Pioneer Zephyr* for the Chicago Museum of Science and Industry, and Scott Brownell, the museum's skilled photographer, took considerable time to shoot photos for us of the restored streamliner on display. The Newberry Library in Chicago opened its Burlington Railroad archives, revealing many of the boardroom machinations and behind-the-scenes memos that shaped the Zephyr projects.

At the invitation of Paul Giblin, a real gentleman, in charge of publicity for the Flying Yankee Restoration Group, we drove to Claremont, New Hampshire, to photograph the Yankee as it resumes its former glory with full operation in mind. The Yankee's basic construction is a virtual clone of the Budd *Pioneer*, Twin Cities, and *Mark Twain* Zephyrs, allowing us to see these trains with "the skin off." Paul also opened their archive to us and followed up with additional material (info@flyingyankee.com). Traveling down to the St. Louis Museum of Transportation, we were allowed to photograph the 9908 *Silver Charger* Zephyr on display amid dozens of fine locomotives and rolling stock. Molly Butterworth, curator of collections, and Nick Ohlman, library curator, helped us get the job done.

To help us trace the Denver Zephyrs, Coi Gehrig of the Denver Public Library Western History Archive worked with us to sort through the huge Otto Perry Photography Collection. In North Freedom, Wisconsin, the Mid-Continent Railway Museum kindly let us photograph two rare examples of pre-Zephyr gas- and diesel-electric motive power in the museum's beautiful and accessible setting.

If you own a Lincoln Zephyr automobile built between 1936 and 1942 you might want to look up the Lincoln Zephyr Owners Club, which sent us photos of their Zephyr and our Zephyr side by side back in 1935. David Cole, the editor of their newsletter *The Way of the Zephyr*, graphics artist Richard Cole, and back-issue distributor Robert Barr all helped us.

Paul Watkins and Jim Carney, excellent model-makers and longtime students of everything to do with railroads, answered a lot of my questions over numerous breakfast sessions. And, finally, my usual collaborator and wonderfully talented writer who took notes, lugged tripods, and endured more railroad jargon than anyone should ever have to absorb, my wife, Janet.

CHAPTER ONE

TESTING SHORT-HAUL DIESELS

General Electric, the American Locomotive Company, and the Ingersoll-Rand company combined their resources to build this demonstration yard-switcher that later became No. 1000 on the Central Railroad of New Jersey in 1925. It weighed 60 tons and was powered by a 300-hp oil-fired diesel-electric engine. Considered to be the first commercially successful diesel-electric locomotive, the yard goat finally shut down its engine for the last time in 1956. Note the cooling grids for the engine on the roof. It was double-headed, with operating controls fore and aft riding on a 24-foot, 2-inch wheelbase. The 36-inch wheels supported 124,000 lbs. (Builder's Photo copy, Gerry Souter Collection)

No great inventions spring to life in a vacuum. These inventions arrive through the confluence of many new technologies. This merging of technologies is fueled by a need, and though the result is often evolutionary over a period of time, its impact can revolutionize a way of life. That's what happened to the Chicago, Burlington & Quincy Railroad, called the "Q" by the farmers, miners, freighters, and passengers who rode its Midwestern rails, as well as the hoggers at the throttles and the flinty-eyed businessmen who ran the show from the boardroom. The Q was big business as a major American hauler of Heartland products and its people, but in the early 1930s, that business was in deep trouble. As the Great Depression that began with the stock market crash of 1929 sucked the life out of the world's economy, railroads began shutting down. Steam engines dumped their fire boxes for the last time, tenders drained their tanks, and tons of rail cars were shunted onto scrap tracks. Thousands of railroaders lost their jobs.

Franklin Roosevelt desperately lunged at every problem with his New Deal to help American industry turn the corner of fear and inaction; however, all the hurts and attempted remedies seemed to work against the railroads. Trucks increased their long-haul freight tonnage over better highways. The infant airline industry bet its future on new airliners like the Douglas DC-1 and DC-2 and the Boeing 247. Railroad passenger service was in decline while busses proliferated for cheap, short-haul passenger travel. Government regulation denied abandonment of unprofitable railroad passenger schedules, and the cost of operation was eating up the railroads' thin-

Early gas-electric experiments were much like this boxy No. 3 "motor" operating for the Montana Western Railroad in 1925. They were familiar on short lines for hauling passengers, freight, and Railway Express to towns that were too small for full-rail service. Built by EMC, the MW No. 31 is powered by a Winton six-cylinder engine, model 106A. Running on gasoline to drive the electric generators, it develops 227 hp. The horizontal shutters control airflow to the gas-engine cooling radiator. Note the operator's controller and the whistle cord. (Courtesy, Mid-Continent Railway Museum, Gerry Souter Photo)

ning margins. The Q carried 18 million passengers in 1924. By 1933, the number had dropped to seven million.

Cut costs, reduce maintenance, trim labor, and increase ridership became every railroad boardroom's monotonous mantra. While freight fed the coffers, passenger service stoked the egos of the great railroads. Passenger travel on short profitable runs with no diner or sleeper service quickly began to lose its luster when hauled by smoky teakettles that spent half their time hung over the grease pit in the roundhouse. Expensive premier service offered signature long-range trains that dueled behind huge Hudson steam locomotives while fast Pacific and Atlantic steamers raced their heavyweight steel passenger cars between city terminals. A railroad's reputation and publicity rode on its passenger "varnish."

Early on in the 1920s when living was good, the Chicago, Burlington & Quincy had invested in a future technology that seemed promising. First

tried back in 1898, the CB&Q had assembled a gas-electric rail car that produced 100 hp at 240 rpm and weighed 12,000 lbs. Unfortunately, 5,000 lbs of that weight was absorbed by a monster flywheel whose sheer torque at that speed caused pieces to fly off the chain-drive transmission like shrapnel. Meanwhile, the clunky three-cylinder gasoline engine ate itself alive as metal crystallized in the high heat. But it was a start. Soon, its improved progeny replaced clapped-out steamers in the railroad's timetables and showed a profit over the many short-haul routes served by the CB&Q.

These gas-mechanical cars were 43 feet long, driven by a 90-hp, six-cylinder gas engine mounted over each power truck. Forty passengers found seats with their baggage, adding to the car's 21-ton weight. Unfortunately for their crew, the twin-engine overloaded hybrid drove like a truck, and often the pair of gas motors didn't synch up properly. At the

Early diesel-electric switch engines used for yard duty, such as this 45-ton model built by Pullman Standard for the U.S. Navy, proved that diesel power plants were reliable, durable, and could be scaled down for railroad work. The early diesels, however, were slow and offered a low power-to-weight ratio. Note the counterbalanced side rods on the two trucks. (Courtesy, Mid-Continent Railway Museum, Gerry Souter Photo)

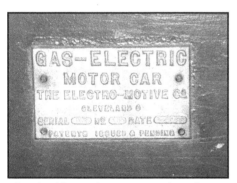

This builder's plate stating the Electro-Motive Corporation of Cleveland, Ohio, built the MW-31 "motor car" in 1925 is affixed below the operator's cab right-side window. Electro-Motive absorbed the Winton Company, builder of the car's gas engine, and went on to become General Motors' Electro-Motive Division. (Courtesy, Mid-Continent Railway Museum, Gerry Souter Photo)

touch of the throttle the two engines took off in opposite directions. Wheels screamed, passengers vibrated, and dense smoke rose above the terminal platform roof. Eventually, the few putt-putt experiments evolved into a sched-

ule of 75-foot motor cars that hauled an RPO (Railway Post Office), Railway Express, baggage, and seats for 24 passengers plus its motive power, a six-cylinder, 275-hp gas engine driving electric traction motors. These "Doodlebugs," with their distinctive horns, became fixtures on the CB&Q's short hauls. They cost just 35 cents a mile to operate compared to 56 cents for a steam engine and boasted an amazing maintenance record of 94 percent availability over a 3.6 million-mile year. That record sent 192 old 4-4-0s and 10-wheeler steamers to the scrap yard. Yes, the Doodlebugs only trundled along at a top speed of 30 mph, but they were cheap and reliable.[1]

By 1927 the CB&Q had begun buying motor cars and trailers from a small replace-and-repair outfit called the Electro-Motive Company working out of an office in Cleveland, Ohio. Electro-Motive subcontracted everything. Car bodies came from Pullman or St. Louis Car, electrical motors and transmissions from General Electric, and its six- and eight-cylinder gas engines from Winton.

By 1930 the CB&Q's experience had ramped up to a Midwest Company 29-foot twin-engine gas-electric locomotive with a steeple cab perched high above and between identical hoods. Beneath the hoods ran a pair of truck-mounted traction motors putting out 330 hp. This type of motive power came to be called "44 tonners" for their weight and the fact that one engineer could operate the locomotive under union rules because it weighed under 50 tons. No. 7168 started life as a yard goat shuffling cars between peddler freights. Soon, it displaced the regular 0-6-0 steam switcher and eventually showed it could haul freight between Keokuk and Mt. Pleasant, Iowa, for $27.95 per round trip compared to $54.77 for a 10-wheeler steam engine. Guess which locomotive ended up as ingots in a gondola?

By now, it seemed obvious that when the financial crises, exacerbated by the Great Depression of the 1930s, began to hit home at the offices of the CB&Q, they had some cost-cutting measures at hand. In 1932 the professorial Ralph Budd took over as president, polished his spectacles, and took a hard look at one of the main reasons they were in this mess.

This graphically simple logo was the herald plastered to the shovelnose of every CB&Q diesel beginning with the 1934 Zephyr through the fleet to the E models, Fs, and FTs. The logo rode on all manner of freight cars and steam-engine tenders until it was recognized around the world as a classy Class-One railroad. (Dave Lotz Collection)

An early Budd railcar, this deeply fluted, wedge-prow experiment ran on 12 rubber tires pushed along with a 125-hp Cummins diesel engine. Power car 4688 and its un-powered trailer rumbled over to the Pennsylvania Railroad for a tryout. Like its sad sister doing a solo act with the Reading Railroad, it was named The Green Goose. (Jim Kerr Collection)

After a trip abroad to find any new ideas and to locate promising diesel engines that might power a rail car, Ralph Budd came home with rubber tires and a Jumo diesel motor to try out. He'd traded a license for his shotweld process to Michelin for the tires. Stuffed into this fluted-steel bus-like conveyance, the Jumo diesel couldn't get out of its own way. The tires slipped off and wore out. The Reading Railroad was the lucky recipient of car No. 65 called The Green Goose. (Jim Kerr Collection)

The most successful pre-Zephyr experiment by Ralph Budd and his designers was the Texas Pacific Silver Slipper. *The 125-hp Cummins diesel was dropped for an American LaFrance 240-hp model that powered true diesel-electric package traction motors. Budd tested the T&P model in Illinois before shipping it to Texas. The name* Silver Slipper *came from its habit of wildly spinning its wheels before starting out due to transmission problems. (Jim Kerr Collection)*

The automobile had bumped many passengers from the ticket booth, so, he reasoned, the internal combustion engine would be used to bring them back.

While at the Great Northern, Budd had supervised the digging of the 7.8-mile Cascade Tunnel in Washington state. One of the longest tunnels in the world, boring and removing material went on non-stop for 35 months. Budd had stationary diesel power plants installed to provide electric power to the workers. The motors' economy and durability made a lasting impression. When diesel power was finally made practical for locomotive installation, he didn't hesitate to purchase a diesel box cab switcher in 1926 for shuttling freight and passenger cars to make up trains. The downsizing of diesel engines had been an industrial quest since Rudolf Diesel received his first patent in 1892.

In 1911 General Electric sent a team of engineers to Europe to explore work going on with diesel-electric power plants. A German firm named Junkers had developed an opposed-piston engine. General Electric licensed five of them for teaming with their own electrical systems to power a series of yard switchers that operated during World

War I. Following the rail industry's great lack of enthusiasm for experimenting with alternatives to steam power, General Electric confined itself to collaboration with other companies to produce diesel-electric motive power.

The Great Northern box cab locomotive that Budd bought resulted from the collaboration between Ingersoll-Rand and General Electric. Ingersoll-Rand built a four-stroke 300-hp diesel engine driving General Electric's electric motors while the American Locomotive Company fashioned the brick-shaped body of a 60-ton diesel-electric switcher. The units were used on 14 railroads, including the Central Railroad of New Jersey, B&O, Lehigh Valley, and the Great Northern. They were cheap to operate, could start a string of heavy freight with the slack out, and ran 24/7 off a sip of diesel. These homely and ponderously slow switch engines proved the diesel-electric concept to any front-office bean counter.

Confirmed by the pile of financial statements stacked on Ralph Budd's desk, the CB&Q's operating income in 1932 had fallen 72 percent from 1931. He had to move quickly.

Two years earlier, General Motors had bought the Winton Engine Company and Electro-Motive, the rail car builder. As Budd pondered that particular synergy, he was also aware that another Budd – Edward G. and no relation – had risen in the fabrication industry after building the first all-steel auto wheel and then producing an all-steel automobile body. In 1932, Edward Gowen Budd had observed the streamlining incorporated in the latest aircraft designs, in particular the Douglas DC-2 and a prototype scheduled for 1935, the DC-3. He wondered if the same principles could be used in constructing railroad cars. Ralph Budd and Edward Budd were on a collision course involving new technologies, the

means to merge them, and the demonstrated need to produce a revolutionary product.

Unfortunately, the first fruit of this inspired collaboration turned out to be a real stinker, but not for want of tinkering about with the right elements. Edward Budd had discovered that stainless steel, with its high 18 percent chromium and 8 percent nickel ("18-8") content, was twice as strong as mild steel, yet could be worked like soft copper. When finished, it was lightweight, naturally shiny, and corrosion-resistant. As a structural material, 18-8 steel sections had been tested for distortion and failure at up to 135,000 lbs per square inch while conventional steel failed at about 35,000 lbs. This allowed the stainless-steel roof and floor of a coach to be structural members capable of resisting stresses that might otherwise need reinforcing girders to offset.

For example, a new stainless-steel coach required some 12,000 lbs of sheet-steel sections – virtually all of it load-bearing. That's roughly the same weight as the central support girder alone in a conventional steel-clad passenger coach.[2] These positive attributes also raised some problems. Stainless steel

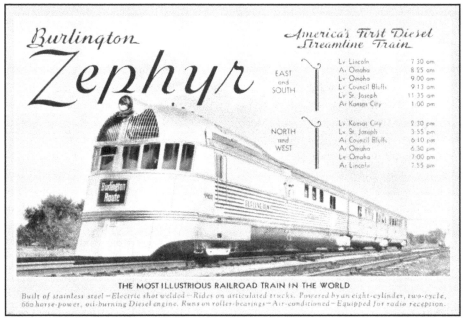

From Lincoln, Nebraska, to Kansas City there was no finer way to travel than aboard the Pioneer Zephyr. This postcard view of the sleek streamliner is complete with a schedule. Advertising boasts of an "oil-burning Diesel engine" and "Electric shot welding." Nontechnical passengers probably appreciated that the Zephyr was "Equipped for radio reception" so they wouldn't miss an episode of Ma Perkins or The Fred Allen Show. (Burlington Route Historical Society Collection)

With its name emblazoned on the rounded "drumhead," the Pioneer Zephyr rolls north across the Mississippi River on a wintry day in 1960. The stainless shrouds that once covered its wheel sets are gone – long sacrificed to easing maintenance. Many new lights and the rear coupler were added later in the train's life as concessions to safety and yard handling. (Jim Neubauer Collection)

Shown operating at North Freedom, Wisconsin, in 1970, the MW No. 31 is the oldest surviving and largely unmodified gas-electric car built by the Electro-Motive Corporation. Residing in the collection of the Mid-Continent Railroad Museum, it is close to as-built condition with its power plant, baggage area, smoking compartment, passenger area, and opposite-end control area largely intact. (Courtesy, Mid-Continent Railway Museum)

was expensive and you couldn't weld it. Application of welding heat rendered stainless steel brittle and charred. The Budd Company turned that problem over to their head engineer, Col. Edward J. W. Ragsdale, to solve. Ragsdale determined that rivet heads in section joinings interfered with close spacing, and punched

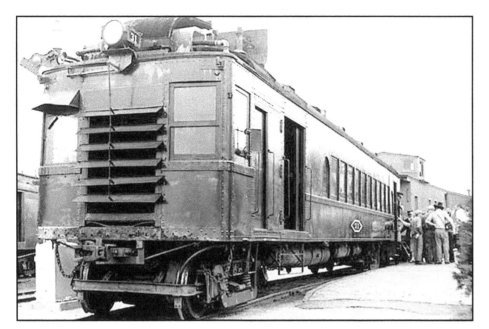

Shown in its striped safety paint job, MW No. 31 was typical of the diesel-electric Doodlebugs used on branch lines and short lines, when a steam passenger train was not warranted. Only two crewmen – a motorman and a conductor – were required to operate the car. It could haul passengers, baggage, and a limited amount of freight. If the ruling grade was not too steep, it could tow one lightweight coach for extra passenger capacity. Most railcars of the 1920s have not survived, being scrapped, converted to trailer cars, re-powered with diesel engines, or converted to rail detector cars. (Courtesy, Mid-Continent Railway Museum, Jim Neubauer Photo)

Budd's Pre-Zephyr Diesel-Electric Rail Cars

At the time, the French tire manufacturer, Michelin, produced a pneumatic rubber flanged wheel. Believing this innovation might be a value-added feature on the developing Budd rail car, the company licensed stainless-steel fabrication to Michelin in return for the tires. To complete his list, Budd secured a German 82-hp opposed-cylinder Junkers Jumo diesel engine for testing and came home.

The combination produced a stainless steel rail car with deep horizontal flutings that raked the body, a sharp-nosed front end, and 12 rubber wheels. It was called *The Green Goose* and looked more like a bus than a railroad car. The Junkers engine turned out to be far too underpowered and was exchanged for an American Cummins diesel at 125 hp. The lot was shipped off to the Reading Company Railroad. Another Cummins diesel was fitted into power car 4688 and, together with an un-powered trailer, sent to the Pennsylvania Railroad. It was the Texas version of this pioneering concept that proved the most successful.

Before shipping the Texas & Pacific rail car back to its home schedule, Budd tested it on Burlington tracks in Illi-nois. The T&P version had its power upped to 240 hp using twin American LaFrance diesel engines over the lead truck along with the traction motors. The rubber tires that occasionally went flat were stripped off the power car, but were left on the matching trailer. This short train looked like it was made to run on rails, clad in shiny stainless steel with large flutings down the sides and a narrow longitudinal pattern on the roof. The front end had a more aerodynamic design and looked less like a snowplow. The power car No. 100 and its rubber-shod trailer, No. 150, were delivered to their run between Texarcana and Fort Worth where the train earned its put-down name *Silver Slipper* by scorching the tracks with wheel spin like it was chained to a post. The Texans shipped the train set back and the bold experiment vanished under the torch.[3]

While the T&P car was being built in Edward Budd's manufacturing plant in June 1933, Ralph Budd finally placed his order for a stainless-steel, diesel-powered speedster for the Burlington. He'd seen enough, and even though the T&P power car was busy grinding notches in Texas trackage, his specs called for a completely different breed of cat.

Designed to be operated by one crewman to stay below a union weight limitation of 50 tons, these diesel-electrics were valued for their low cost of operation and pulling power. This locomotive runs on two Cummins NH150 diesel engines generating 300 hp each. They power one electric motor for each truck that is connected by side rods. They were slow, but remained in many yards until World War II and more powerful SW and NW models emerged. (Courtesy, Mid-Continent Railway Museum, Jim Neubauer Photo)

holes took away steel and weakened connections, whereas electric spot-welding of the period seemed to work with 18-8 steel. In an article in the April 14, 1934, *Traffic World Magazine*, Ragsdale is quoted on his new "Shotweld Process."

"In making a 'shotweld,' two or more sheets are held together by oppositely placed electrodes and a current is passed between them. Resistance offered in the current path causes heating and, eventually, local fusion between the sheets. Here, (the weld) has an elongation of 65 percent and, what is of further importance, a shear strength of 75,000 lbs per square inch. Both are approximately twice the equivalent values of a steel rivet."

Lighter shots of electrical current could be used since stainless 18-8 steel had 8 to 10 times less resistance than standard carbon steel to achieve a local weld 3/16 inch in diameter. That same 18-8 steel was used in the flanged box sections that formed the truss members with a tensile strength of 150,000 lbs per square inch. A sheet 0.050 inch in thickness was compressed in a test from a 14-inch-long section to a length of 6-3/4 inches without breaking. Ragsdale's team developed a portable shotweld unit that could be easily repositioned throughout the construction, and Budd Manufacturing patented the process.

The expense of stainless steel forced consideration of cost savings to make the

cars and their operation profitable. Since weight of the units had been trimmed, two additional possibilities were immediately evident – reduce the weight of the engine without cutting its power, and reduce friction on the track to increase speed. As for fuel costs, Edward Budd knew that diesel-powered stationary plants had proved diesel engines could run on hair tonic if necessary, but the big problem was the weight of the engine estimated in lbs-per-horsepower. In Europe, the birthplace of the diesel engine, diesel technology was far advanced over American producers, so Ed Budd headed overseas with a shopping list.

CHAPTER TWO

BUILDING THE
FIRST ZEPHYR 9900

The trucks on the original and subsequent three-car Zephyrs were shrouded in stainless steel to complement the streamlining effect of the stainless underbellies of the cars. With fewer surfaces to catch the wind, the Zephyr's aerodynamics allowed the cars to slide through the air and hug the rails. Like virtually all shrouding experiments tried by the railroads, the maintenance time required to pry the shrouds off whenever work had to be performed more than outweighed aerodynamic priorities. Over time, the Zephyrs lost their shrouds. (Scott Brownell photo, courtesy, Museum of Science and Industry, Chicago)

n his own words, Ralph Budd's stated goal was to seek "…situations where a train had to be operated where earnings were insufficient for any profit."[4] As mentioned earlier, Budd had great familiarity with diesel power plants but hadn't yet seen one that answered every need for rail motive power. All of the ones Ed Budd had tried – Junkers, Cummins, American LaFrance – had severe downsides. In September 1933, Ralph had even journeyed to Philadelphia and taken a ride on Ed Budd's *Green Goose*. His impression was mostly negative, but the stainless-steel construction reduced maintenance to a pittance. The concept of a short, lightweight passenger train was sound. More than 25 percent of all passenger revenue on the CB&Q was generated by short hauls operating two five-car trains powered by steamers or gas-electric Doodlebugs. He liked the direction Ed Budd was heading and on June 17, 1933, Ralph Budd unscrewed his fountain pen and signed the Budd Manufacturing Company's bid to build this short, light, high-speed, highly profitable little train. He left all the details up to Ed, except for one. Ralph Budd specified a Winton diesel engine for the power plant and then went back to the CB&Q to await developments.

During the late 1920s, the Winton Engine Company had pressed on trying to meet the railroads' insatiable need for more and more horsepower, as well as the demands placed on Winton's prime contractor, the Electro-Motive Company. There was no way, with the gasoline engines of the time, that more power could be squeezed from the carburetor-based spark-plug and air-mixture system. Also, as gasoline consumption increased with automobile and airplane use, cash needs to build new refineries and distri-

bution systems were passed along to the consumer in higher prices per gallon. Diesel power needed only cheap stove oil and air. The heat of compression alone fired the cylinders. But the resulting engine was a comparative behemoth chugging along at 60 lbs of engine weight per horsepower.

In 1930 an automobile maker, General Motors, inhaled both the financially strapped Electro-Motive Company and Winton Engine. A new player entered the game in the person of GM's vice president of research, Charles W. ("Boss Ket") Kettering. Winton's president, Harold L. Hamilton, and Kettering turned their focus on producing a light-weight diesel for the railroads.

Three years passed before the team and GM's research department produced a pair of identical working prototypes of the 201 diesel engines. These two-cycle in-line diesels produced 600 hp with eight cylinders. Winton's earlier power plants required four cycles to complete the intake-compression-fire-exhaust sequence.

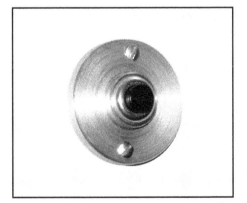

Enunciator buttons were available for passengers to call the steward(s) in the buffet grill. This button was behind a drape in the restored Pioneer Zephyr's lounge observation or parlor car. (Scott Brownell photo, courtesy, Museum of Science and Industry, Chicago)

This package of piping carried water that helped cool the Pioneer Zephyr's Winton eight-cylinder engine. Most cooling racks were mounted on the roof of early box-cab diesel locomotives, but Budd designers did not compromise the Zephyr's streamlined design. They used the slotted space around the stacks to suck out the breeze blown into the engine room by the enormous fans behind the Zephyr's grillwork, cooling the water in the pipes to cycle back into the engine. (Scott Brownell photo, courtesy, Museum of Science and Industry, Chicago)

The first stroke sucked in fresh air that was compressed by the second stroke. An injector shot in a squirt of fuel on the compression stroke that ignited and shoved the piston down into its power stroke. The last stroke, exhaust, cleared the burned fuel out the exhaust port valves. With a two-cycle engine, the fresh air was blown into the cylinder with a power blower as the

This art deco brass grill cover on the restored Pioneer Zephyr *marks the location above the door where the Stromberg Carlson radio once resided. Music, live sports broadcasts, and entertainment shows were piped to the cars through a series of built-in speakers. Later in the Zephyrs' life cycle, conflicts of passenger programming demands required installation of a wire recorder that played prerecorded music. (Scott Brownell photo, courtesy, Museum of Science and Industry, Chicago)*

One of the drop-leaf lino-covered end tables in the lounge parlor car was a landing space for drinks or reading material in this "first-class" section of the Pioneer Zephyr. *Next to it is one of the dozen unbolted chairs that lined the wall. Throughout the Zephyrs' style changes, these chairs were tinkered with – trimming a half-inch off the back legs for instance – to make them more comfortable. Also visible is one of two floor heating ducts that lined both sides of the cars. The chrome obstacle is to restrain visitors who tour the restored* Pioneer Zephyr. *(Scott Brownell photo, courtesy, Museum of Science and Industry, Chicago)*

exhaust blew out. In a four-stroke, every other piston downstroke was a power stroke. In comparison, a two-stroke produces power with every piston downstroke.

One of the Winton's key innovations was the unit injector. It allowed solid fuel (unmixed with air) to be fed into the cylinder under thousands of pounds of pressure. The injector's big advantage was that it eliminated the need for high pressure in long fuel lines. The unit injector, which was also a pump, created the pressure at the moment fuel entered the cylinder.[5]

GM shipped the pair of Model 201 engines to Chicago for the 1933 Century of Progress Exposition. Their final bench test was to drive a replica of a GM assembly line for the two-year run of the show.

The ever-curious Ralph Budd was poking around Winton's Cleveland plant when he first saw the two engines being built. He immediately recognized their potential. The bench test at Chicago, where the venue was spotless and the engines were bolted down to a cement floor, was hardly comparable to the raucous, vibrating, dirty, hot environment of a locomotive at speed. Budd asked Kettering for the engines anyway.

Kettering and Hamilton admired Budd for his spunk, but knew a long frustrating shakedown was ahead for the exposition models. They suggested Budd should wait until the bugs were shaken out. Budd could only see the Union Pacific's M-10000 streamlined locomotive taking shape across the continent in the race to get the world's first streamliner on the track. Averill Harriman, the UP's chief, was laying the whip to his engineers. Budd gave in to GM's caution, but he still specified the Winton engine for the new train when he accepted Edward Budd's bid that year.

In 1951 Kettering confessed in a speech to the American Society of Mechanical Engineers about Electro-Motive's pioneering in diesel engine design, "…This casting carried the overhead camshaft, as well as the passages

The 40-seat passenger space is shown here with mannequins to give a sense of scale in the original Pioneer Zephyr. While the colors are faithfully matched, the two speaker enclosures flanking the door would look good fronting today's modern sound systems. Note the absence of overhead racks. The first Zephyr had none, but raised seats to 18 inches above the floor to allow for packages. (Scott Brownell photo, courtesy, Museum of Science and Industry, Chicago)

for cooling water, fuel, and lubricating oil. When the (Winton 201) engine was first started these three liquids came out almost every place except where they should. After resorting to doping, peening, and everything in the book, the first engine was finally made to run… To mention the parts with which we had trouble in Chicago would take far too much time. Let it suffice to say that I do not remember any trouble with the dip stick."

Ralph Budd said later, "I knew that if General Motors was willing to put the engine in a train, the national spotlight would be on the corporation. They'd simply have to stay with it until it was satisfactory. I knew they'd make good. Actually, I wasn't taking a chance at all."

The opportunity to shake down the 201 engine at Chicago's Century of Progress fair allowed GM to create the Winton 201A. The new engine weighed only 20 lbs per hp compared to 60 lbs for the first two-cycle engine, provided 80 hp per cylinder, and had a predicted cylinder life of 80,000 miles.

The final engine design that was lowered into the body of the Zephyr was a unique machine according to Ralph Budd's description in the April 1934 edition of *Traffic World Magazine*:

"The Zephyr is the first motor-car train in this country to utilize the two-cycle diesel engine as a prime mover. This engine has eight cylinders; 8-inch bore by 10-inch stroke, and develops 600 brake horsepower at 750 revolutions per minute. Without generator, it weighs 13,428 pounds or 20.8 pounds per bhp. A two-cycle slow-speed marine-type diesel engine, turning at over 104 rpm, weighs 216 pounds per bhp. Four-cycle diesel engines used in some oil-electric freight locomotives in this country operate at 550 rpm and weigh approximately 31 pounds per bhp. Four-cycle gasoline engines, such as are used in rail motorcars, operating at 950 rpm weigh at 24.6 pounds per rpm."[6]

On earlier diesel switch engines, their low-rev engines never developed many heat problems due to their slow top speed. Radiator cells that carried away the heated water from the engine cooling jackets were perched on the roof. The new Zephyr, however, was designed to be a "speedster." Cooling this two-cycle, high-rev engine putting out 1,000 degrees at the cylinder head during compression to achieve the

The Rival Union Pacific M-10000

Averill Harriman's Union Pacific Railroad found itself in a race with the CB&Q to put the first lightweight, diesel-streamlined train on the tracks. Like Ralph Budd, Harriman also saw the streamliner as a savior for the dying railroad passenger service. In 1935, 85 percent of Americans with enough spare change in their pockets to afford a vacation drove to their destinations in automobiles. Harriman spared no efforts in luring travelers to his railroad either by innovations such as his M-10000 streamliner or later on, developing the Sun Valley, Idaho, ski resort as a great family vacation destination.

The M-10000 was also an articulated train, but made of aluminum instead of stainless steel. The Pullman Car Company had received the building contract and Winton had been chosen to supply a diesel 201A engine. The Union Pacific streamliner was a far less innovative (read "risky") concept than the CB&Q train, but it caught the public's attention as the time drew near for its debut. Harriman feared Budd's streamliner might steal the M-10000's thunder if the stainless-steel train rolled out of the shop first, so an executive decision changed the Winton order from an experimental 201A diesel to a proven 191A V-12 distillate-powered engine.

The planned operation of the two trains was as different as their designs. The Union Pacific chose to target long-distance runs between the West Coast and Chicago while Budd saw the Zephyr as taking over a short-haul day trip of 500 miles serving Lincoln, Omaha, and Kansas City. The M-10000 had installed an auxiliary 191A Winton engine as back-up motive power in case of long-haul problems.

With a great whoop of publicity and drum beating the M-10000 rolled out two months ahead of the Zephyr. The yellow and brown Union Pacific streamliner named the City of Salina blazed across the newspapers and newsreels as the first streamlined train (if you don't count Budd's Texas & Pacific rail car of 1933). Newsweek magazine's unkind review called it "a great bulbous-headed caterpillar." A commemorative coin made of the same aluminum used in the train's construction was issued by the UP, and cross-country tours with attendant celebrities covered 13,000 miles.

Although subsequent Model 10001 and 10002 articulated trains running Winton 201A diesel engines were put into service by the Union Pacific, when World War II broke out in 1941, the trains' aluminum was worth more as scrap. They were pulled from service and torched while the Zephyr-type, in one form or another, continued running into the 1960s.

explosion that drives the piston back down for 750 revolutions per minute required considerably more cooling surface. Also, placing the radiators on the roof spoiled the aerodynamics of the slick steel hull. So engineers attached the radiators to the interior ceiling above the engine. To feed an artificial stream of wind that carried off the radiated heat, two large grills were set into the Zephyr's front end above the cab windows. These "eyebrows" that adorned every shovelnose power car drew in air that was augmented by a pair of fans driven by the main engine through belts. The huge volume of air passed over the radiator grillwork and up out of the car through a longitudinal slot in the roof. Engine exhaust manifolds fed their gasses out through stacks also set in the roof.

In a gas-mechanical rail car, the engine drives the wheels directly through a geared transmission like an automobile. In a gas- or diesel-electric, the power is transferred to the wheels by way of electrically driven traction motors. The Zephyr diesel engine crankshaft was turned by the pistons that in turn spun GM's GT-534 main generator putting out up to 750 volts of power into the truck-mounted motor assembly, and three CP-127B-11 motor-driven air compressors. The traction motors powered by the GE generator were connected to the wheel axles by gears. When more traction motors were attached to more axles, the result was higher traction effort and greater pulling power.

Beneath the Zephyr, only the front truck had one pair of GE model T16 traction motors attached to the axles of its four 36-inch wheels. No traction motor blowers were employed due to the self-ventilating design. The 30-inch rear truck shared the weight of the baggage car in the articulated setup and was "free-wheeling." This arrangement worked fine for the Zephyr's short three-car train. Later, as the trains grew in number of cars to meet demand, additional diesel engines and power trucks were needed.

In addition to powering the big GE generator that ran the traction motors, the Winton diesel also operated a belt-driven GT1177A-1 auxiliary

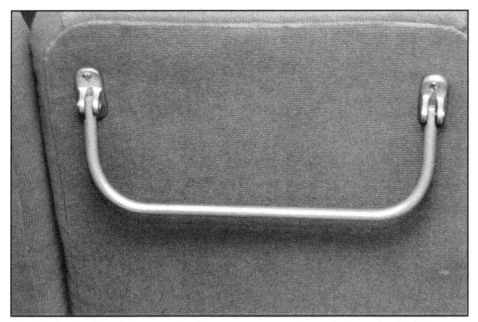

76-volt generator for lighting, air conditioning, heating, boiler, battery charging, train controls, buffet utensils, and other miscellaneous odds and ends. Its speed was kept constant from idling to full engine speed by a new type of dynamic relay.[7] In an essentially electric-powered locomotive loaded down with electric pumps, lamps, toaster ovens in the passengers' grill, and

On the back of each Pioneer Zephyr *seat was a robe rack through which the passenger slipped his or her overcoat or suit jacket. There were no overhead racks and scant space for briefcases or small hand luggage. Eventually cup holders and hat clips were installed, culminating in overhead racks bolted in place, besmirching the designers' wished-for uncluttered look. (Scott Brownell photo, courtesy, Museum of Science and Industry, Chicago)*

Practicality ruled in this section of the Pioneer Zephyr. The residue of tobacco smoke was easily sponged from the leather seats. The floor was brown linoleum. You can imagine this car full of men in shirtsleeves, hurtling along at 90 mph, puffing two-for-a-quarter cigars, ice clinking in their whiskey glasses, listening to Max Baer getting the tar beat out of him by James J. Braddock on the Stromberg Carlson radio. (Scott Brownell photo, courtesy, Museum of Science and Industry, Chicago)

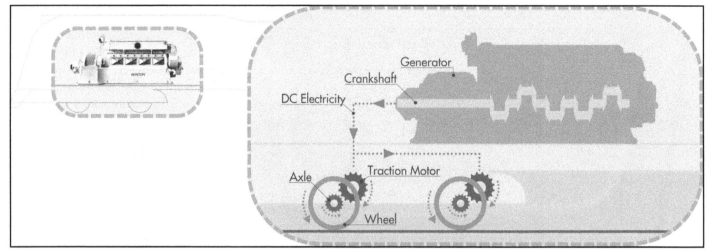

This graphic demonstrates the power transfer that turns the crankshaft with the Winton 201A's pistons to spin the electric generator which, in turn, sends direct current (DC) to the electric traction motors on each axle of the locomotive's power truck. The traction motor's gears mesh with gears on the axle to turn the wheels. (Graphic produced by the Museum of Science and Industry, Chicago, and reproduced with their permission)

Working room was at a premium in the confines of the Pioneer Zephyr's *engine room. Looking forward toward the engineer's cab, the big Winton eight-cylinder diesel engine is flanked by electric cabinets, the oil cooler, and other machinery. Facing are twin lubricating-oil pressure gauges for either side of the motor. With the engine hammering, the big fans howling air into the compartment, and the various pumps whirring, conversation must have been difficult at best. (Scott Brownell photo, courtesy, Museum of Science and Industry, Chicago)*

environmental accessories, batteries take on considerable importance. A 64-volt Exide Ironclad with 32 cells delivering 450 ampere-hours when rated at the 10-hour discharge rate sat in a stainless-steel battery pit in the engine room. This behemoth weighed 3,200 lbs when ready to turn over the engine and power up the auxiliary circuits.

When a standard steam-powered locomotive was designed, it was a self-contained unit concerned with its own propulsion, providing air to the brake system, steam to heat passenger cars, and electricity for its own lighting. Passenger cars each carried their own generators, battery boxes for lighting, and reservoirs for water. Steam heat for passenger cars that did away with dangerous coal stoves or circulating hot water was introduced in 1881. The Baltimore & Ohio placed in continuous service the first mechanically air-conditioned passenger coach in 1930. On May 24, 1931, the B&O began operating the world's first completely air-conditioned passenger train.

One of the Zephyr's advantages of being designed as a unit allowed for maximum efficiency in the design and placement of these basic amenities needed for the harsh swings of Midwestern weather. However, besides being a test bed for its designers, the Zephyr had to perform under the public scrutiny. Even though their first route only covered 500 miles of track, every detail had to operate so as to pamper the 72 encapsulated passengers. Climate control was required to be a transparent feature.

Prairie winters were often long and severe, so the steam heating system required flawless operation. Looking like a whiskey still, an all-too-common sight in recently post-Prohibition America, with its vertical Peter Smith boiler surrounded with coils of copper tubing and

This diagram of the back end of the Pioneer Zephyr *shows from the left: The steam generator in the baggage space, the unique buffet grill, a 20-seat smoking car, 40-passenger coach seating, and the door leading into the "first class" lounge-parlor-observation section with its chairs following the curving wall contour. Note the entrance-exit door separates the coach from parlor seating and the two lavatories in the parlor section. At the very rear of the car is a writing desk and lamp that were later replaced by an emergency exit for obvious reasons. (Courtesy, Railway Age)*

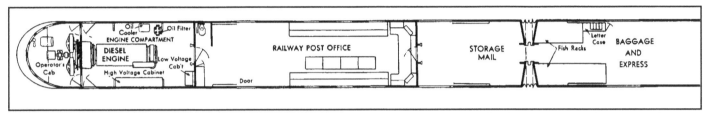

The front end of the Pioneer Zephyr *was all business. One seat for the engineer, a place for the Winton diesel engine and its support systems, a railway post office with a hands-and-knees door into the mail storage area, and a door into the next car opening into baggage and railway express space – a practical blend of motive power and revenue generation. (Courtesy, Railway Age)*

wearing a conical top hat, the system, built by the Vapor Car Heating Company of Chicago, was tucked away in a corner of the baggage space across from a 50-gallon feedwater storage tank in the train's second car. The oil-fired system required 75 gallons of fuel. It operated automatically providing 500 lbs of steam per hour at a pressure of 85 lbs per square inch.

The heater's automation came from four controls. Three electrodes were dunked in a water column attached to and fed by the boiler that reflected the amount of water available for conversion to steam. The long electrode monitored when the water had dropped to a low and dangerous level as soon as the wire was uncovered and lost its 110-volt DC circuit. When it did, the oil-supply valve and the oil-burner motor were shut off. The mid-length and short electrodes determined the water depth between them and turned the water feed pump on or off to maintain the correct level to keep steam flowing.

The fourth control came from a pressure switch that measured boiler pressure. If that pressure became too

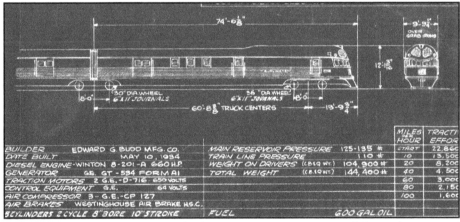

This blueprint of the Budd design for the Burlington Zephyr *gives all the vital statistics of the power car from nose to diaphragm. Note the head-on view drawing has the locomotive "scowling" to a greater degree than the final product's gentler "frown" caused by the slightly angled grillwork above the cab. (Burlington Route Historical Society)*

high, the switch reduced the oil flow and the burner flame was reduced down to a minimum. When pressure dropped to the correct level, the burner was re-ignited and its flame restored.

Heat was sent to the passengers by a pair of finned tubes. One tube passed through the evaporator unit in the air conditioner that added heat to the fresh and re-circulated air. This air was distributed through ducts to the passenger

compartments. A second finned tube transported steam heat to radiators mounted at floor level on both sides of each car. Automatic valves, controlled by thermostats mounted halfway up the walls, regulated distribution of the steam.

Water condensate from the radiators drained into a pair of small sumps. As the float in the sump rose, a switch tripped, releasing air pressure into a separate pipeline that recycled the condensate

A close-up view of one of the engine-room fans used to draw air through the pair of forward grillworks above the cab's front windows. The air helped cool water in the pipes that lined the compartment ceiling as part of the engine-cooling system. Normally, those pipes would be on the roof, but the streamline design required them to be inside and thus the necessary fans. (Gerry Souter Photo)

In construction of the 9900 and the Flying Yankee, the use of folded and tubular stainless steel as lightweight but very strong support elements is shown here in the parlor car. No heavy beam-work was required due to the weight loads being spread throughout the car structure. With no "roof" or doorway lintels as such, the downward weight stresses were minimized. (Gerry Souter Photo)

From the inside of the fluted steel wall, we see diagonal supports shotwelded directly to the gussets, creating a stronger bond with the vertical extruded wall supports. Using steel throughout in this fashion helped with both strength and flexibility of the structures. (Gerry Souter Photo)

into the feedwater storage tank in the baggage car.[8]

Summers on the Great Plains were no bargain, either, so ample provisions had to be made for cooling the cars.

Grilles above the connecting doors let in the air cooled by separate York mechanical air-conditioning systems for each car. Both compressors and evaporators were located beneath the floors. The circulated air exited the cars through filter-protected exhaust openings located in the floors above the evaporator units.

The Zephyr possessed all the climate comforts of home, but in such an ultra-modern environment they were expected to. The Zephyr's biggest bragging rights came from its capability for high-speed runs. Streamlining and weight loss governed almost every decision except safety in the construction process. The unity of the train through articulation was one of those decisions.

By the 1930s, articulated locomotives were fairly common. These big steam engines were really two locomotives combined into one. All drive wheels and their pulling power were laid on the rails without the expensive expe-

diency of actually having to hook two smaller engines together, called "double heading." Articulated motive power was achieved in two ways. A "simple" articulated engine had two sets of pistons driven from the same boiler mounted on a hinged frame with the steam split between two sets of driving wheels. The Whyte wheel designation might be two pilot wheels followed by eight drivers followed by a second set of eight drivers and a two-wheel trailing truck, or 2-8-8-2 (Chesapeake & Ohio H-7, 1924). The other was the Mallet, a "compound" locomotive, which tied together a high-pressure engine in the rear to a low-pressure engine in the front with a hinged arrangement beneath the same boiler. Steam use was maximized by sending

Looking forward across the top of the Winton engine with its header removed, we can see both engine-room fans and one set of interior grillwork that covered them. The fans resided above and behind the engineer's cab, providing cool air for the Winton's engine-cooling system. (Gerry Souter Photo)

internal-combustion engine had slashed into steam-train revenues, the auto manufacturers' adoption of Art Deco's flowing lines from the 1920s made contrasting rail passenger cars look dumpy and out of touch. Auto sales had plummeted after 1929, and the changeover from dowdy, four-square car designs to new tear-drop shapes began increasing showroom traffic. What made these new cars more attractive also made them more efficient.

Decreased air resistance, better brake and engine cooling, reduced gas consumption, better visibility – a long list of engineering plusses made the new autos more appealing to male buyers. Female buyers, a growing demographic, appreciated the style and futuristic lines of not only autos, but toasters, refrigerators, vacuum cleaners, and household decoration. Prewar women had also begun their rise toward increased empowerment with more and more purchase decisions from the family budget.

the steam, once used, from the high-pressure cylinder up to the low-pressure to be used again. The hinged locomotives could be accommodated on tighter radius curves, which was a plus in mountainous regions.

Articulated passenger cars were an entirely different animal. The concept had been tried on trolley cars with limited success – hinging two cars together over a single center truck to expand capacity. Both Budd's and Harriman's design teams hit on the articulated train solution for their innovative streamlining concepts. Both the CB&Q and the UP would stretch the idea of a unit train to its maximum practicable limit until the limitations outweighed the advantages. In 1933, those advantages appeared to be very compelling.

For the Q, short-haul passenger service needed a kick-start to stop the cash drain and the new look, streamlining, had caught fire as an economic confidence-builder. Just as the automobile's

Custom-extruded and roll-formed stainless-steel channels create a web of support for the steel roof. These channels conform to the curvature of the roof and are shotwelded in place to become part of the roof structure. This construction process removed the need for heavy, load-bearing elements found in standard passenger cars. (Gerry Souter Photo)

During restoration of the Flying Yankee, *it was discovered that each window had been custom-fitted into its space. A window from the other side of the car would not slide into another space without modification. The windows rode in a flexible putty base that allowed the glass and its support to flex with high-speed turns and withstand vibration. Each window comprised two glass panes, an air space, and plastic sheet to prevent shatter in case of impact. (Gerry Souter Photo)*

The Zephyr and its West Coast rival were natural extensions of that stylistic trend. The flowing line of the short fast train was a marketing stroke at a time when safe aerodynamic airliners were still in their infancy.

Since speed was also a major requirement, streamlining gave the *appearance* of speed even when standing still. To disrupt that appearance with diaphragms connecting square-ended coaches perched high on standard trucks detracted from that image of slicing through the wind. Even the name "Zephyr" (see sidebar) suggested rapid transit.

The Budd Manufacturing Company designers chose to drop the cars down onto equalized, swing-motion cast-steel trucks with a very long 8-foot wheelbase and six-inch Timken roller-bearing journals that were hollow-bored to shave a bit more weight. The powered lead truck had 36-inch wheels and a gear ratio of 52:25. To minimize wind drag, the trucks were sheathed in stainless-steel housings.

Noise was a major concern to the designers. With the coach windows

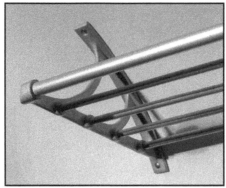

The original Zephyr was designed to provide hand-baggage stowing space beneath the seats by allowing additional under-seat room. By the time of the Twin Zephyrs *and* Flying Yankee *in 1935, passenger needs required overhead stowage. Everyone wore hats in the 1930s. Hat clips were tried on the backs of seats, but crossing your legs booted your hat into the aisle. Women's hats were especially vulnerable. Both the* Twin Zephyrs *and the* Yankee – *and later on, the* Pioneer Zephyr – *came equipped with these Art Deco-inspired overhead racks. (Gerry Souter Photo)*

sealed against wind and outside noise, clatter of the wheels crashing over track joiners, grade crossings, diamonds and switch points carried up through the trucks and bolsters to the coach floor. To counter the click and rumble of track noise, rubber insulation was applied liberally wherever metal-on-metal facing occurred. Oilite metal inserts were vulcanized onto the truck pedestals and bolsters where the steel surfaces pressed down on the truck frames. Oilite is a bearing or insert made of oil-impregnated bronze or other porous metal. The kingpins that form truck pivots were also treated. Any rigging rub points on the truck were faced with brake lining, and all spring sockets and bearing points contained Oilite metal elements.

Because of the radically different functions of the three cars, none of the trucks carried the same load. But because the train was designed as a unit, the loading retained the same ratio of wear from front to back.

Removal of the name-plaque panel between fluted steel sections on the side of the Flying Yankee *reveals tubular-formed stainless-steel supports running diagonally and vertically down both sides of the car. This provided lightweight strength and rustproof durability. (Gerry Souter Photo)*

Ralph Budd stumped into his office straight from the train on which he'd come from Chicago and the 1933 Century of Progress Exposition. It was a hot spring afternoon and, as was his usual practice, he had to see for himself the diesel engines that were proposed to run this new train. They were two 600-hp Model 201A Winton diesels built by John Kettering and his team of engineers. Budd had been so impressed watching them operate the GM exhibit, he wanted the pair shipped to Ed Budd's manufacturing facility and one of them stuffed into the new power car as soon as the exposition was over. Kettering had known the engines were spurting oil and squirting precious fluids in all directions and suggested patience. Grousing with impatience, now Budd faced another decision.

Waiting for him were three executives: Edward Flynn, Fred Gurley, and Albert Cotsworth. These old railroad hands settled around Budd's desk to plan the new train's run. Eventually they decided the diesel-electric would begin its life on the 295-mile route between Kansas City and Omaha with a stop at Lincoln. The steam-hauled train currently running that schedule was losing money by the sack

"... when Zephyrus [the west wind] blows sweetly on the tender shoots in every forest and heath, and the young sun has run halfway through its course in the sign of the Ram...then people long to go on pilgrimages..."

— *Geoffrey Chaucer*, The Canterbury Tales

full, but the government demanded the service be continued.

With the diesel-electric's route decided the meeting broke up, all except Al Cotsworth who stayed behind. He asked Ralph one question.

"What will we name it?"

The train would obviously make a splash in the newspapers and newsreels, so the CB&Q publicity mill had better prepare ahead of time with a catchy name. Since their train was the last word in rail transportation, Cotsworth wanted to look up the last word in the dictionary and see if it fit. Budd picked up his office dictionary, paged to the back and found, "Zymurgy: the practice and art of wine making, brewing or distilling." The *Burlington Zymurgy* was hardly suitable. Further dictionary searching gave no satisfaction.

At home, Budd had been reading Chaucer's *Canterbury Tales*. He thumbed through the book until he found "Zephyrus, God of the West Wind." A phone call to Cotsworth sealed the deal; the new train that would become a legend deserved a legendary name. The publicity department began loading up on their new star, the *Burlington Zephyr*.

Power truck (36-inch wheels)	98,000 lbs.
First trailer truck (30-inch wheels)	67,000 lbs.
Second trailer truck (30-inch wheels)	45,000 lbs.
Third trailer truck (30-inch wheels)	30,000 lbs.

Every design element of the Zephyr seemed aimed at making it go faster by being lighter and sleeker and slipping through the air pushed by a fast high-power engine. As shown in the Prolog, going 100 mph had been done back in the 1890s. By 1934 any well-maintained Class 1 steam engine designed to couple prize company varnish to its drawbar could, on any warm summer day, given a straight stretch of flat track, top out over 100 mph punching white smoke from its stack like a machine gun. But the division bosses hated it.

Big steam locomotives running at speed pounded the daylights out of the most heavy-duty rail. Time lost to track maintenance more than negated some highballing hogger with his throttle tied down. And worst of all, more crews and passengers met their Maker while running too fast. The Zephyr, on the other hand, was designed for speed. Passengers experienced a giddy anticipation climbing aboard something as big as a train knowing it had the ability to propel them as fast as a race car. Louis Meyer had won the 1933 Indianapolis 500 Mile Race at a speed of 104 mph and that was with a driver and mechanic in one car. The Zephyr was geared to fly at 117 mph, carrying 72 passengers, their baggage, and the US Mail, while serving up a toasted cheese sandwich and cold ginger ale as riders tore across the prairie.

To that end, a lot of thought went into the Zephyr's brakes. Here again, the Zephyr's uniqueness was both a problem and a feature. The Westinghouse SME-3 brake system couldn't be installed

Articulation was a major part of the Zephyr/Flying Yankee concept since it removed the need for additional wheels and their weight and friction on the track. To achieve this, Budd used this connection shown on the end of the Flying Yankee's *parlor car restoration in progress. The system operates with a basic male-female (female shown here) drop-in pin supported with an open fork casting. (Gerry Souter Photo)*

right out of the box without being modified for the articulated train. Besides operating the brakes in the closed train system, allowance had to be made for the occasional times the Zephyr might have to be towed by a steam engine. Three brake lines were operational.

The first brake line was the emergency pipeline that maintained the levels of the on-board air reservoirs. If any reservoir dropped its pressure below a certain level, valves would automatically apply the brakes. The second straight pipe regulated control valves that adjusted gradual brake application and release, and the third line connected to a steam locomotive's air system when a tow was needed. The second pipeline actually controlled the Zephyr's brakes during regular operation. A handle directly in front of the motorman regulated the air pressure with great sensitivity. In the center of the handle was a button that had to be held down while the train was in motion. When released, this electro-pneumatic "dead-man" control, together with a pneumatically operated foot pedal, caused shutdown of all power and applied the brakes.

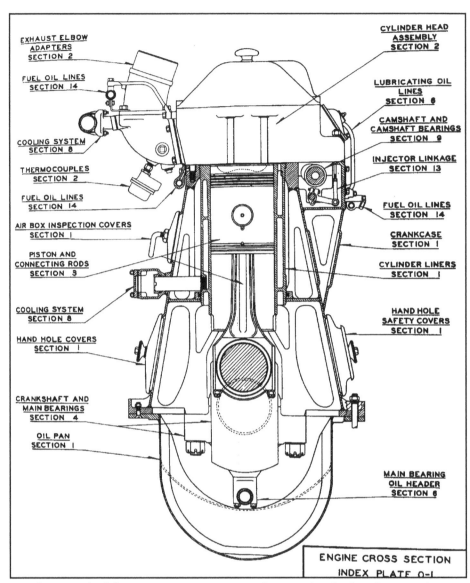

As photographed from a rare maintenance diagram book, this drawing shows a cross-section of the Winton 600-hp diesel engine that powered the CB&Q Pioneer Zephyr, *the* Twin Cities Zephyrs, *and the Boston & Maine* Flying Yankee. *(Gerry Souter Photo)*

Besides this dead-man control, the Zephyr was fitted with an innovative form of "governor" that provided automatic brake retardation that could be preset. A pendulum moved along the line of train motion and detected acceleration and deceleration, opening and closing a battery circuit with its motion by engaging magnets in each car's braking system. Lights flashed on the motorman's console letting him know that the preset governor was engaged. Years later, a similar system would provide a simple readout on paper

to show when and where a hogger might have "let 'er rip" and violated the right-of-way speed limit.

Like other operating systems on the Zephyr, this elaborate composite brake system with its valves, brake cylinders, and other fittings relied on aluminum to hold down weight. The air reservoirs, like the truck shields, were made of corrosion-proof stainless steel.

The original Zephyr, the *Pioneer Zephyr*, had a good safety record up to October 2, 1939, on the way from

Looking from the rear of the power car, the Winton engine and its annealed steel bed virtually fill the engine compartment – and this is with major components still on the shop floor getting individual attention. The two cooling fans above the engineer's cab are clearly seen, but many lube oil and water tanks, as well as the electrical cabinet, are missing, as is the floor on either side of the engine bed. (Gerry Souter Photo)

Kansas City to Omaha. It was zipping along the Missouri River when the brakeman for a way-freight, waiting on a through-siding for the *Pioneer Zephyr* to pass, misread "open" for "close" and threw a switch in front of the streamliner. The silver shovelnose whizzed onto the siding at 50 mph head-on into an iron steam locomotive squatting there with its loaded freight cars. The unfortunate motorman on the *Pioneer Zephyr* was mixed in with the wreckage halfway back into the RPO section of the power car. An accompanying roadmaster riding the right seat died later, but no passengers were seriously injured. The construction of the power car absorbed the entire impact of the 50-mph-to-zero event. Within two months the entire train had been rebuilt and returned to service.

Budd's construction techniques foreshadowed later "crush zones" in the shell that covered all the other systems. Unfortunately, the motorman's cab was placed in the very front zone, a design error that led to the eventual demise of the shovelnose concept. The cab-forward placement also had other problems, as we'll see later.

The Budd engineers employed a mix of materials more familiar to the aircraft industry than railroads at that time and, combined with the shotwelded stainless-steel components, one construction innovation led to the next.

Earlier passenger cars had been framed up like building a house with a sturdy floor bolted to I and T girders, and load-bearing walls supporting a roof perched on top. The Zephyr, on the other

A line of 3/8-inch-diameter shotwelds runs down a stainless-steel fold-over form that abuts the steel flooring in the parlor car. These shotwelds and processes Budd developed and patented were key to the ability to work with durable, 18-8 shiny stainless steel created originally by the Krupp Steel Works in Germany. With shotwelding, Budd created what one writer described as "...the modern age of metal fabrication, and snatched the lead in developing what would become one of the most prized 'miracle metals'." (The American Experience – PBS) (Gerry Souter Photo)

A particularly good view of the custom-shaped forms folded and shotwelded to both gussets and shaped angle brackets. This illustrates the fabrication possibilities to meet any special circumstance such as supports passing through a wall and still maintaining their functional integrity. (Gerry Souter Photo)

hand, used Pratt truss side frames made of box sections created by deeply flanged channels held together with shotwelds and extending up to the roof by diagonals between the windows. This method joined the roof to the entire structure with steel sections gauged at 150,000 lbs per square foot minimum tensile strength. Combined with the 75,000-lb-per-square-inch shear strength of the shotwelds, the walls and roof formed a steel cocoon that surrounded passengers. The design came very close to the safety result offered by modern monocoque construction in high-performance automobiles where epoxy-joined body panels of fiberglass or aluminum formed the key part of the structure's overall strength.

Stainless-steel sheeting formed the Zephyr's corrugated floor, which was welded to 11 stringers, which were, in turn, connected to transverse supports. These elements joined together to create a floor that simulated a stiff girder, transferring its end loads to the side-wall girders and capable of loading 600 pounds per linear foot. The end result of the unified floor, walls, and roof was a tube with great structural integrity. While a standard passenger car normally employed heavy girders integrated with the truck bolsters for wall and roof buttressing as well as below-floor equipment support, the trussed center sills beneath the Zephyr floor acted only as equipment connection points and local reinforcement.

One piece of equipment that needed a particularly sturdy connecting point was the Winton diesel-electric engine. The Winton's engine bed was fabricated of arc-welded steel plate rather than cast, and then annealed in high heat and cooled to make the final piece less brittle. An integrated form 25 feet, 3-1/2 inches long by 8 feet, 8 inches wide, the bed also served as the power car's front bumper and truck bolster. The Lukens Steel Company provided their patented Chromansil, an alloy that combined chromium, manganese, and silica into a form with a 90,000 lb tensile strength.

As the parlor car wall warps to create a rounded back end to the observation car, the fluted stainless steel conforms to the same shape. The formed and extruded channel supports, joined at sheet gussets to the floor and the anchor ring that follows the window ledge, also warp. Note the floor is also stainless steel (originally above Masonite underlament). (Gerry Souter Photo)

The 6,070-lb multipurpose component fitted into the floor side trusses and provided a base for the power car's unique nose support. With the exterior steel skin off, the Zephyr's front end was a rounded cage stiffened at its center by a center member that reached up from the apex of the bumper and engine bed to the hairline of the roof. Horizontal steel belts followed the contour of the bumper's wraparound and were supported by raked vertical members that also anchored the window frames for 180-degree forward and side vision for the crew. The nose member also supported the headlight and the contoured steel panels that formed the roof. Grilles flanked the center arched beam like frowning black eyebrows, behind which were the fans carrying forced air to the diesel engine to carry away heat and aid the Roots-type blower in achieving proper fuel combustion.

The Zephyr's nose points up a unique exterior distinction between it and the stainless-steel cars previously built by Budd. Wind-tunnel tests of the train completed at the Massachusetts Institute of Technology demonstrated that aerodynamic results were improved by using 1/8-inch-thick, contour-following, non-fluted, stainless-steel panels wrapped around the enormous proboscis. Non-fluted sheets of steel 0.030 inches thick formed the roof sheathing above the motorman's cab and the engine room. The deadlight panels between the windows were built up of sheets of plywood sandwiched between stainless steel and copper sheathing. These "Plymetl" panels were unusually strong because of their bonded composition. They resisted warping as they slid into channels, held in place with a non-hardening caulking compound. Non-fluted stainless was also wrapped around the rear of the streamlined lounge car to improve air flow and reduce swirling suction that forms behind stub-ended trains, acting almost like a trailing parachute to retard speed.

Completing the interior finishing of the streamlined tube was the further isolation of track noise from all the compartments. Corrugated sheeting was placed below the floor level and insulated from the interior flooring by hair felt stuffed between 80-lb sheets of craft paper glued to the sheeting surface. A material called Alfol, made of a multilayer reflective insulation and having an inside layer of 0.00045-inch aluminum foil, was used to pack between the Masonite walls, while the roof was headlined with Agasote pressed-paper heat insulation. Where interior decoration was not a high priority, such as in the mail and baggage rooms, galvanized sheets covered the walls and floors insulated with thin cork cemented to the sheeting and layered with roofing paper. The mailroom floor received an additional layer of one-inch-thick sanded maple to deal with heavy foot traffic and bag scuffing as the letter and package sorting process took place between station stops.

With all three cars having their skins on, what finally made them truly unique was the articulation process that held them together. As mentioned earlier, articulated transport experiments mostly occurred with trolleys. These attached, multiunit "motors" were never designed to be separated, just hauled out to service high-traffic schedules and then shuttled back into the barn.

Realistically, an articulated passenger train had to expect separation from time to time as maintenance dictated, especially when increased demand required longer trains (as eventually happened). Articulation of the Zephyr cars was achieved with end-frame articulation castings attached to the car frame with the only rivets used in the cars' construction. A pair of these castings was linked above a single four-wheel truck. Since the cars rode so low to the track, standard coupler heights for all other railroads were too high for the Zephyr and the trains that followed the articulated concept. A standard knuckle-type coupler was available to be manhandled to each Zephyr power car's front end and attached to a fixture behind

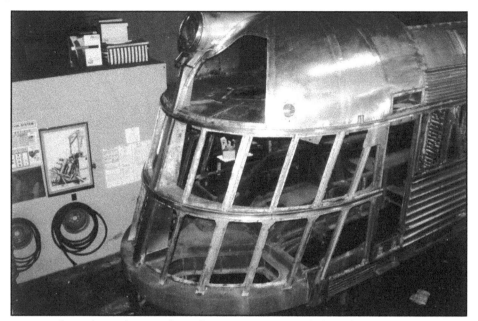

An excellent photo showing how the one-piece annealed steel nose support-engine bed-front truck bolster relates to the stainless-steel cage supporting the operator's compartment. The welded steel front end was the single heaviest component in the Zephyrs. (Courtesy, Flying Yankee Restoration Group)

Having been lifted from the bed in the Flying Yankee power car, the Winton diesel engine lies ready for a major overhaul. The eight pistons are still in place. (Courtesy, Flying Yankee Restoration Group)

a removable plate so a steam or diesel switcher could tow one of the shovelnoses to a maintenance track or facility.

With the various mechanisms installed in the Zephyr's three-piece "fuse-lage," the people interfaces come next. Like the mechanical elements, the system controls and passenger amenities soaked up considerable thought from the engineers and designers. Of all the persons aboard the Zephyr, the hardest working and most critical was the engineer, or motorman as the early diesel-electric hoggers were called. The most famous motor-man associated with the Zephyr series was Jack Ford, one of three who "piloted" the Pioneer Zephyr on its famous speed run from Denver to Chicago.

The "uniform" of a locomotive engineer had been frozen in time since the one-piece denim bib overall first found its way into a steamer's cab. Most railroad men in the days of steam left their work clothes hanging on a peg in the round-house locker room until the reeking garments could stand by themselves from the layers of grease, coal dust, and ash. They were considered to be properly broken-in at that time. Riding in the cab of a coal-fired muzzle-loader was dirty business, but layers of grime and hardened patches of dried sweat were the badge of a veteran. Jack Ford and the other motormen, however, always looked like they'd just stepped off the 18th green at the country club. A white shirt, necktie, and a jaunty flat cap would have gotten any of them frog-marched out of the roundhouse 20 years earlier. But this was the dawn of the diesel drivers; even their coveralls made them look more like lab technicians.

The Zephyr's cab appeared to any grizzled steam hogger like it belonged on the 4th Avenue trolley. No Johnson

Winton 600-hp diesel engine sits on two skids on the shop floor with its eight pistons drawn out for reconditioning. The color of the piston chambers indicates there is a lot of work ahead. (Courtesy, Flying Yankee Restoration Group)

Looking wretched, seven of the eight Winton pistons drawn from their engine just prior to a strip-down overhaul lie on wood strips awaiting series cleaning. Every element of the Flying Yankee *requires stripping and rebuilding to make the train safe for full operation. (Courtesy, Flying Yankee Restoration Group)*

Looking forward across the top of the 9900 engine compartment reveals the big Winton 600-hp diesel engine on its bed and the pair of fans that blew cooling air through grillwork on the front of the power car. Below right is the entry into the engineer's cab. Virtually everything was new to the Budd designers as they created this streamliner. (BNSF Photo)

bar, no clusters of valves and dials, no grate shaker, blower, water glasses, or firebox scissor doors. One of the few recognizable items was the whistle cord. The greatest challenge, however, was the view. Jack Ford had a 180-degree view of the track ahead and to both sides. His controls were all within reach as the engine roared at his back.

Actually, the generator was directly behind Ford as he sat in the only seat with the majority of controls to his left. The Westinghouse air-brake module dominated the center of the cab with the dead-man brake control jutting from its circular track. Beneath the control's handle, looking like a bicycle handlebar brake, was a sand-release valve. The air brake's pressure gauge sat in the middle of the cab's three primary gauges, flanked by the combination engine-cooling-water and oil-pressure dial on the left and the speedometer to the right. Levers that controlled idling speed, engine speed, and the forward-reverse controller handle were all to Ford's right. The whistle cord hung from the ceiling and looped around a crank handle that opened the top half of one of the two opening front windows. Beneath the automobile-like "dashboard" was the cab heater. There was no seat for a fireman. A second crewman seemed redundant to the original designers what with the few necessary controls, the 180-degree field of view, and automatic operation of most systems. Eventually, however, due to safety considerations, the seating capacity for crewmembers grew to three abreast on the final Zephyr power car, the *Silver Charger* of 1939.

While the rest of the Zephyr's passengers traveled in relative quiet, the engine compartment/motorman's cab was a noisy workplace with the eight-cylinder engine hammering away, the generator whining at Ford's back, and the two large fans above and behind his head blasting wind from the front-end grilles back across the engine's air

9900 stretches sinuously down a track alongside the Budd Manufacturing Company in 1934, looking like a silver dragon with its "scowling" air intake grills above the windows. The design at this stage was simple and uncluttered. Over the years, it morphed and grew, stretching out to 15 cars and loading up on steroids in the engine room, but the first pure shovelnose concept always remained recognizable. (BNSF Photo)

One-Piece Welded Engine Bed

The nose support, power truck bolster, and engine bed were built in one piece – not cast but created by layers of steel annealed by heat treatment and welding into a solid piece. This gave the front end great rigidity and complemented the stainless-steel shell that formed the car's structure with no heavy load-bearing beams required. (BNSF Photo)

intakes. The whistle had a high-pitched fluting tweet that belied the rich grumble of the diesel power plant.

Behind the 8-foot-deep cab, the big Winton diesel was housed in a 16-foot-long engine compartment with very narrow aisles on both sides. Just past a battery cabinet, a doorway opened into the 30 feet of space allotted to the Railway Post Office. There, mail was collected at the stops by a sack and through a slot in the shiny steel exterior. Postal employees then sorted the mail, and bags were stored in the 16-foot mail storage space. From the mail room where a couple of busy clerks flipped envelopes into slots and open bags supported in frames, a small 24-inch creep door under the sorting shelf opened into the 30 feet of baggage and express storage.

The next door passed between the power car and the combine car (baggage and passenger), protected from the elements by a pair of flexible exterior

diaphragms. The footplate between the cars was circular and rode in a pair of slots, allowing the cars to pivot over the single supporting truck. A circular brass plate was in the center, allowing for inspection of the coupling system. At the far end of the baggage and express space and directly behind the steam-heat boiler was a steel bulkhead shielding the buffet grill. Here, stewards prepared drinks and cooked hot sandwiches and other light meals with electric appliances. Virtually every surface, from where food was prepared to the vertical icebox and refrigeration lockers, was stainless steel. Waiters took the food from the counter into the first passenger space, which had seats for 20 travelers who could eat off cantilevered tables that slid into cast slots in the seats. This was also the smoking car.

A second passenger door, protected by exterior diaphragms and bridging the cars with another pivoting footplate,

allowed access to the 40-seat passenger section and its semi-reclining chairs. Following the aisle to the rounded rear of the train was space for a dozen inward-facing armchairs, wall-mounted swing-up tables, bolted-down cigarette ash trays, and a writing desk with a desk lamp for this first-class "solarium lounge."

Access to the passenger compartments from the station side was through hinged doors and fold-down steps. Stepwells reaching the exit steps were covered with fold-up trapdoors when not in use. All the exterior doors were flush with the stainless-steel car sides providing an unbroken streamlined airflow. Sliding stainless-clad doors slid open for access to the baggage and mail compartments. When the Zephyr began its scheduled service, the RPO car exit door was fitted with a standard mail pick-up arm for collecting mail sacks on the fly.

The overall mechanical and aerodynamic design of the Zephyr was the work of many designers and engineers. To act as advisors, the architectural firm of Holabird & Root was brought on board by the Burlington, but design concept honors went to a young aeronautical engineer from the Massachusetts Institute of Technology. The ink was barely dry on Albert Dean's graduate

The original parlor car at the back end of the 9900 Zephyr was a pocket rendition of the old-time opulent observation cars, all paneled and plushed. By 1934, plush was at a minimum, but the Budd designers still managed to make the "salon" seem elegant with the separate chairs, weighted smoking stands, lino-covered drop-leaf tables, and gold draperies. One wonders if the writing table in the very rear was ever used. (BNSF Photo)

degree when he joined the Budd Manufacturing Company. His contribution has been deemed responsible for the overall exterior look of the Zephyr and her resulting progeny. Following the automotive industry's lead, he recognized the application of aerodynamics and ground effects, using downward air pressure on the raked front end and contoured roofline to press the low-slung Zephyr into the tracks at high speeds. The underside of each car was also shrouded with stainless steel to allow a smooth stream of air to slide beneath the speeding train.

The interior design of furnishings, color schemes, and passenger amenities, however, went to the design firm of Paul Phillipe Cret of Philadelphia. He graduated from the Ecole des Beaux-Arts in 1903 and was serving as consulting architect for The University of Texas at Austin when hired by Budd to work on the train's interior. Cret's liaison with the Budd team was another Beaux-Arts-trained architect named John Harbeson, who would go on to win many awards for his work and become Cret's partner. The result of their collaboration with Budd's designers was an elegant interior treatment for the CB&Q's passengers.

The great signature trains of the 1930s offered private compartments, barber shops, smoking lounges, bars, and diners with four-star-quality food, telephones, and secretaries and typists for business travelers. Steam engines and individual cars cost a fortune to design, build, and maintain. Class 1 railroads, like the Chicago, Burlington & Quincy, New York Central, Pennsylvania, Illinois Central, Union Pacific, Atchison Topeka & Santa Fe, Milwaukee Road, Wabash, and others, maintained their prestigious high-profile passenger schedules regardless of the flow of red ink. To catch the attention of profitable short-haul day-trippers, a degree of luxury had to replace the second-class equipment used to squeeze every dime from declining revenue.

The CB&Q Railroad and Budd Manufacturing were not the only folks seeking high-speed passenger rail service. Harte H. Diggins of Woodstock, Illinois, invented the Velocitor, a streamlined train capable of traveling 125 mph. It was a single-unit car designed with comfortable passenger accommodations, air conditioning, sound-proofing, and freight storage. Air pressure channeled across its "ground effects" prow, much like modern sports cars, would hold it to the rails. It also had a rudder. The Velocitor never developed past the model stage because the Burlington Zephyr was introduced and was deemed more practical for modern railroad use. It is on display at the McHenry County Historical Society Museum in Union, Illinois. (Courtesy, McHenry County (Illinois) Historical Society, Gerry Souter Photo)

Harte H. Diggins is shown revealing his Velocitor on March 27, 1934. The high-speed train design was competition for the Burlington Zephyr. It was designed to carry passengers, freight, and Railway Express at speeds up to 125 mph. The Velocitor concept utilizes air pressure to hold it to the rails much like modern sports car "wings." The power plant could be diesel-electric, gas-electric, or Diggins' own "hydraulic drive." A rudder mounted at the stern could be "steered" to minimize flange pressure on high-speed turns. (Courtesy, McHenry County (Illinois) Historical Society, Gerry Souter Photo)

RIGHT: The Pioneer 9900 spent 40 years parked in front of Chicago's Museum of Science & Industry, becoming the decaying home for stray cats. It was shuffled around to the side of the building so the U-505 German submarine could stand alone. Here it is with the stainless-steel sheath removed from the steel "cowcatcher" support welded to the one-piece truck bolster-engine bed. (Photo courtesy, Archives, Museum of Science and Industry, Chicago)

The Q was competing with its own high standards created for the prestigious passenger runs.

The overall theme of the passenger car interiors matched the stainless-steel exterior that mirrored and softened the colors of its surroundings. Pastel shades were used throughout the cars. Pale wall colors beneath cream-colored ceilings complemented the upholstery, window curtains, and floor coverings. Ornamentation was limited to stainless and aluminum banding and the use of brushed aluminum wherever bare metalwork was shown. Exquisite details were often cast in brass, such as the door holders in each vestibule – small sculptures in their own right.

The 20-chair smoking section featured brown leather chairs flanked by walls in pastel rose with curtains of golden rose. Due to the need for constant cleaning of tobacco-smoke residue, the floor was laid with dark and mottled Armstrong Linotile™ squares. Apart from the utilitarian décor of the smoking section, the 40-passenger chair portion of the last car was given a softer treatment.

The passenger compartment theme was quiet repose. Riders reclined in armchairs upholstered in gray-green low-pile mohair with a hint of gold in the fabric's background. Walls of warm gray touched with green flanked the chairs. Chase Seamlock carpet in taupe covered the floor, and the windows were curtained in pale green silk to match the upholstery. The rear of that coach, separated by two doors and the lavatories, comprised the

Looking down the length of the 9900 Pioneer Zephyr *in captivity at the Museum of Science and Industry in Chicago, it's easy to see the smooth stainless-steel roof with panels screwed in place for ease of engine removal. This front hump sloped down to the fluted steel roof that covered the three cars. The four stack ports face rearward on the roof spine. (Photo courtesy, Archives, Museum of Science and Industry, Chicago)*

solarium lounge, and the color/lighting theme picked up from quiet to active for cocktails, writing, and conversation.

Wall color shifted to a pale gray blended with a tinge of purple-blue. Here the lounge chairs' purple-blue with a gold background mohair acted as accents to the lighter wall color and were further enhanced by the gray Seamlock carpet and gold-draped curtains that lined the walls, showcasing each window's view. Coach lighting came from indirect (reflected) light sources concealed in ceiling-mounted ducts, giving an overall soft glow and eight candlepower illumination at reading height. The solarium lounge differed in that the lights, showing through frosted glass panels that ran along the bottom of the fixtures, were more direct above the circle of armchairs. Air-conditioning grilles were placed above the doorways, and on either side of the end bulkheads a pair of loudspeakers played radio programming tuned in on a Stromberg Carlson 11-tube receiver in the conductor's charge. Passengers could listen to music or news from Gabriel Heatter or Walter Winchell. Comedians Jack Benny, Bob Hope, and Fred Allen brought the laughs, and drama programs such as *Grand Central Station*, *Ma Perkins*, or the *Lux Theater of the Air* made time fly.

Formica covered the lounge's blue side tables, and their folding leaves were decorated with aluminum striping. At the very back of the car resided a half-round writing desk illuminated by a narrow desk lamp. All the windows that circled the lounge area were unshaded since this was an observation car. Coach passengers had the option to pull down their neutral-colored Pantasote™ window shades. This material offered a unique surface coating that withstood exposure to diesel exhaust residue and hair oils. The trade name was used generically for surface-coated, double-texture coverings and became one of the

favored choices of auto makers for their convertible tops well into the 1930s. The exterior color of all the window shades was an aluminum finish to match each car's polished stainless-steel sides.

Additional carry-on stowage was provided by designing each aluminum chair to have a high floor clearance for storing hand valises, hat boxes, and briefcases. Each chair semi-reclined and had both a "robe bar" for overcoats and a spring clip to hold a hat attached to its back. Everybody wore hats in the 1930s. For other baggage that could be gotten to quickly, racks were built into either side of the short passage between cars. These thoughtful touches eliminated the cluttered overhead racks above the seats and the hazard of airborne missiles in case of heavy brake applications. However, passengers' affinity for lugging stuff eventually eroded this "clean, uncluttered" look in future Zephyrs. Overhead racks soon made their appearance.

Just aft of the engine-room bulkhead, a toilet behind a simple partition and draw

This is the buffet grill where a steward used electric appliances to make snacks, beverages, and light meals for 72 passengers. The doorway leads to the baggage compartment and the square above the door once housed the Stromberg Carlson 11-tube radio whose programs were piped through the cars. The grill provided everything from two-for-a-quarter cigars and cocktails to hot sandwiches and ice-cream sundaes at 90 mph. (Photo courtesy, Archives, Museum of Science and Industry, Chicago)

curtain was installed for the crew with another one across from the steam heater and next to the bulkhead, separating the baggage and express from the buffet grill. A single lavatory with a built-in sink served the 20-passenger smoking compartment while the 40-passenger compartment and 12-passenger lounge had two gender-specific lavatories complete with stainless-steel sinks and vanity tables with one porcelain urinal for the gents.

The buffet grill was literally sandwiched between the baggage compartment and the car's entry/exit vestibule. The grill's functional design demonstrated a remarkable use of space for one or two stewards who prepared and delivered a short menu of hot and cold drinks, snacks, lunches, and light dinners to seated riders or as take-away from the buffet's narrow counter. Removable black Formica trays locked into cast fittings at each seat for dining or card games. Virtually all surfaces in the "kitchen" area were stainless steel for

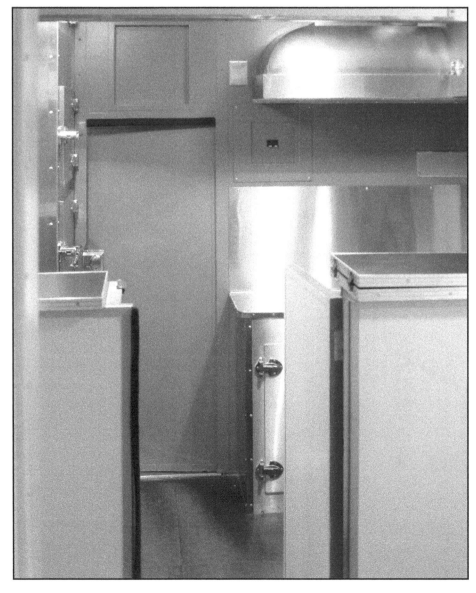

A closer look at the buffet grill in the 9900 Pioneer Zephyr shows stainless-steel surfaces and Formica countertops. Coffee urns and electric hot plates sat on the steel surface beneath the exhaust hood. To the left were cabinets for ice, ice cream, and other refrigeration units. Later Zephyrs enlarged this tiny space into a full kitchen and added stools to the counter-front. (Photo courtesy, Archives, Museum of Science and Industry, Chicago)

A Buffet Grill Menu — 1934

Breakfast

Tomato, Prune, Pineapple or Orange Juice	20¢
	20¢
Grapefruit, Half	10¢
Orange, Whole or Sliced	25¢
Dry Cereal with Cream	25¢
Eggs Fried or Scrambled	
Dry or Buttered Toast with Jelly/Marmalade	10¢
Sweet Roll or 2 Doughnuts	10¢
Coffee (cup)	10¢
Individual Bottle of Milk	10¢
Coffee or Cocoa (pot)	20¢

Lunch/Dinner

Ham/Cheese Sandwich	20¢
Hamburger	20¢
Hot Dog	20¢
Fried Egg Sandwich	20¢

Baked Beans, Hot/Cold with Brown Bread	30¢
Spaghetti with Tomato Sauce	25¢
Lettuce-Tomato Salad	25¢
Fruit or Shrimp Salad	35¢
Bread & Butter or Toast	10¢
Strawberry Preserves	20¢

Grapefruit, Half	20¢
Individual Pie	10¢
Ice Cream with Cookies	25¢
Individual Bottle Milk	10¢
Coffee, Tea, Cocoa (pot)	20¢
Coffee, cup	10¢

Lemonade Glass		
Orangeade Glass	Split	15¢
Ginger Ale	Pint	25¢
Apollinaris Water	3 oz.	10¢
	Split	20¢
	Pint	30¢
White Rock	Split	20¢
Lithia Water	Pint	30¢
	Bottle	25¢
Ale	Bottle	25¢
Beer	Individual	25¢,
Whiskey		40¢,
		50¢
	Individual	50¢
Brandy	Individual	25¢
Gin	Individual	35¢
Cocktail		
		5¢,
Cigars		10¢,15¢,
		2 for 25¢
		15¢ & 25¢
Cigarettes		(Not sold in Iowa)
	Pack	40¢
Playing Cards	Individual	15¢
Bromo Seltzer		25¢
Aspirin Box 12		

Courtesy: Chicago Museum of Science and Industry

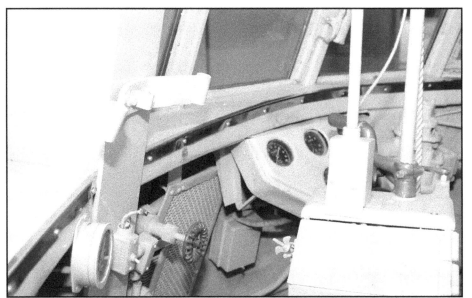

The design of the original Pioneer Zephyr *called for one motorman to sit on the right side of the cab with all the necessary controls. The generator intruded into the compartment, leaving little room for a fireman or trainmaster. During the Zephyr's record-breaking run, three or four rubbernecks often crowded into this space, but didn't stay long as the scenery shot past at 100 mph. The brass idling-speed control can be seen on the other side of the center box. (Photo courtesy, Archives, Museum of Science and Industry, Chicago)*

ease of cleaning. Simple button-push enunciators located throughout each car alerted the grill steward that a rider desired some service.

Looking into the grill kitchen from the entry/exit vestibule revealed the refrigerator cabinet. This was located on the left beneath the swing-up ceiling-height hatch of the ice chute that led down to an ice chest. Next came a 22-inch-by-60-inch door to the baggage compartment After that came the electric griddle next to the coffee urn and a water boiler, all on a work surface above a storage cabinet. The built-in Stromberg Carlson 11-tube radio and its accompanying speaker were located above the door with the control knobs that tuned in the programming from the National, American, Columbia, and Mutual Broadcasting Networks.

The right side wall had a window, an 18-inch-wide work surface, and more cabinets and drawers. The counter-top then spanned the kitchen with a fold-up 20-inch-by-43-inch section for front access in the counter's center. Included in that surface was a sink and a drain board for dealing with dirty dishes. Beneath the sink was a heating radiator grille, since cold breezes could come in from the open vestibule doors at station stops. Beneath the end of the counter-top closest to the refrigerator wall there was a wet-towel bin, ice-cream storage, a brine tank, and crushed ice next to the water-cooler. The refrigerator wall also had a window and another 18-inch-wide preparation surface.

This efficient cubby hole reflected the latest Modernism of the 1930s Art Deco look. A relevant example of this style was the Hotel Overview in New York, located one block from today's United Nations. The 26-story building, built in 1928, is an Art Deco landmark. To commemorate the streamlined passenger trains of the 1930s, the hotel created its own compact Art Deco *Zephyr Grill* on the main floor for quick breakfasts and hot snacks.

As the train hurtled along at 90 mph, food arrived at the passengers' seats on dishware designed specifically for the Zephyr. To minimize storage room, the cream-colored dishes decorated with gold bands and the CB&Q emblem had only a half-inch rim instead of the usual two-inch edge to allow for closer stacking and to fit on the serving trays.

Of course, the big attraction to riders flying down the tracks munching a chicken sandwich was the view. Not even the window glass was ordered off the shelf. Pittsburgh Plate Glass Company provided safety glass for every aperture, but it had to be specially formulated from standard glass used in automobile windshields. Because of the high speeds attained, the plates had to be much stronger but not any heavier. This challenge resulted in a special glass that was 15 percent lighter than conventional panes, but also much stronger. Safety glass is a sandwich of actual glass on either side of plastic sheeting that provides its strength. For the Zephyr's safety glass, this meant thinning the actual glass from 7/64 to 0.09 inches and thickening the plastic sheet from 0.025 to 0.050 inches for the side and rear windows and to 0.075 for the cab windows.

Changing glass formulation can cause other problems. To keep the stronger glass from discoloring, a special anti-ultraviolet plastic was used and the glass itself chemically enhanced to block virtually all ultraviolet rays. Twice the protection did maintain the glass clarity up to the restoration of the *Pioneer Zephyr* for the Museum of Science and Industry display in the 21st century.

A clear view, however, is no advantage if the glass cracks under severe stress caused by the stainless-steel body flexing around high-speed curves and weaving through a yard full of switches. Standard hard glazing was not the answer, so the glass panels were set in a non-hardening putty that had the consistency of Play-doh®, called "dum-dum putty." This material secured the panes of safety glass, but flexed along with the channels that held the windows in place along the car sides. Each window was individually hand-fitted.

Finally, the Zephyr had to have eyes of its own, especially up front. The motorman had to see way down the track under all conditions as the train ate up those high-speed miles. The front headlight housing was faired right into the roofline and peak of the front and center arch between the two eyebrow air grilles. The reflector housing on the *Pioneer Zephyr* contained a 14-inch-diameter Golden Glow unit by the Electric Service Supplies Company that put out 250 watts. This configuration changed over the years of service to include new advances in track illumination and warning systems. The Zephyr fleet added oscillating "Mars" lights, dual lamp housings, and multiple bulb units. Each generation of shovelnoses took advantage of the latest available technology to maintain its edge over competition.

The last touches were its name and number boards. The Burlington had numbered all its internal-combustion engine locomotives and miscellaneous "motors" in the 9000 series. Locomotives started at 9000 while the self-contained gas cars bore number boards starting at 9450. The Zephyr had been awarded an RPO mail contract and had sizeable baggage capacity so it earned a 9700 number. But there was nothing like the Zephyr anywhere, so one whole number group was skipped and the famous 9900 mirror-finish stainless-steel number board was affixed to the power car's fluted side. On the nose went the owner's shield, "Burlington Route," and she was done.

This control cluster is a spiffed-up version of the original, more Spartan setup. From left to right we see the idling-speed controller, the engine throttle, forward-reverse controller, floor-heater grill, and gauges for water temperature, oil pressure, air brake pressure, and speed indicator. The Westinghouse brake column on the right has been deactivated by the restorers, removing the brake grip, dead-man button, and rail-sander release. (Photo courtesy, Archives, Museum of Science and Industry, Chicago)

CHAPTER THREE

THE ZEPHYR STEPS OUT

the PIONEER Zephyr

America's First Diesel-Powered Streamlined Train...

Over the life of the Zephyr fleet, the CB&Q's PR department cranked out a mass of publicity pieces showing off the Zephyr to the riding public. This one came out in 1939, a year after the last Zephyr, the 9908 Silver Charger, took to the rails. Union Pacific's M-10000 was the first streamliner, but the Zephyr was the first diesel-powered streamlined train. By this time, the Pioneer had been seen in different roles all over the CB&Q system. (Dave Lotz Collection)

Eventually, the last workshop tweaks and tests were finished, and everyone at the Budd Manufacturing Company downed tools and stepped back to see what they had accomplished. The *Burlington Zephyr* was like nothing ever seen before on rails. To grasp the Zephyr's visual impact on April 7, 1934, the day it was rolled out of the factory, you only had to park it next to the most modern steam engine in the yard; let's say a 4-8-4 Northern, arguably the most efficient, popular, long-lasting steam-locomotive class ever built.

The Northern locomotive and its tender alone were as long as half the entire Zephyr train. Both ran on flanged wheels and both had headlights. Each one had a door to the engineer's cab. The comparison stopped there. A second look at the Northern locomotive showed that every working part of that steamer could be found on any steam engine built in the 19th century. In that locomotive, railroad designers had optimized steam motive power and there, parked next to its massive bulk, stood the Budd Zephyr looking more like a toy than a revolution. Some rail tests lay ahead to see if the little train's performance matched the futuristic image.

Just two days after being hauled onto the track outside the plant, the as-yet officially un-christened diesel-electric train rolled down the ladder tracks out onto a cleared section and clicked along through Philadelphia until it passed the Broad Street Station. The throttle control was inched forward, sliding around its quadrant. Heading northwest along the Pennsylvania tracks, following the banks of the Schuylkill River, the silver train received green boards and pointed its shovelnose at Perkiomen Junction, Pennsylvania, 24.8

Still in its prime, the 9900 Pioneer Zephyr clips along beneath an overpass at Wataga, Illinois, a railroad town north of Galesburg. The Zephyr's original headlight proclaims the diesel is still in revenue service. The view also gives a good look at the Winton engine's exhaust stacks protruding through the roof. It seems a roadmaster or other CB&Q employee has squeezed into the right side of the cab. (Jim Singer Collection)

miles distant. Drivers on State Route 23, where the river pinched in toward Valley Forge, found themselves trying to keep pace with this silver streak rocketing along the familiar tracks. It blew past them at 104 mph.

On April 17, 1934, the Zephyr officially joined the Chicago, Burlington & Quincy Railroad in a ceremony at Philadelphia's Broad Street Station. The station platform was crowded with guests, politicians, and the two Budds. A virtual

American Flyer Duels Lionel with a Zephyr Model

(Adapted from *American Flyer*, *Classic Toy Trains*, Gerry and Janet Souter, Friedman/Fairfax, 2002, NYC)

Lionel, the famous maker of toy electric trains, had been bird-dogging the Union Pacific Railroad for exclusive use of their plans for the M-10000 streamliner, a distillate-electric train being built by Pullman with a Winton distillate-powered engine. These specs were turned into an O-Gauge 1/45 scale model designed to run on Lionel's new wider-radius O-72 three-rail track.

At the same time the Budd Manufacturing Company began construction of the *Burlington Zephyr* prototype in 1933, American Flyer designers got the green light from their owner, Ogden Coleman, to begin creating an O-Gauge model of the diesel-electric competitor. Realizing the importance of publicity, Budd and the CB&Q readily approved the joint effort and gave Coleman the plans, keeping the toy-train company up to date as designs fluctuated.

While Lionel chose die-casting and sheet steel for its M-10000, American Flyer's production solution involved casting the Zephyr in aluminum using sand molds. Flyer's project manager, Simon Chaplin, had tried using tin-plated steel, but the required shiny appearance ended up getting badly scratched in the production process. Since Flyer's die-casting vendor explained the company's die-casting machines were incapable of producing the desired shells, sand molds were the only remaining solution. Using these molds required considerable grinding. Each train component was cast in two halves and fused together down the roof center lines.

Budd kept changing the train's contours and each change required American Flyer designers to re-do their own molds. These molds were changed eight times until the final design was locked down in 1934. As aluminum bodies arrived at American Flyer's Chicago plant, drum grinders with oilstone surfaces cleaned up the rough centerlines while the final polishing used jeweler's rouge on buffing wheels. Plastic films were affixed over window ports, braces were attached at the floor level, and spring-loaded coupling tabs joined the articulated cars together. After a final polishing, and the affixing of decals and ornamental skirts attached over each articulated truck, as with the prototype, the model 9900 American Flyer Zephyr was ready to roll down the three-rail main line.[9]

The final shipped version for 1934 offered the two-car train and a power car. For some reason a manual reverse lever was affixed to an impossible position beneath the skirt of the power car. You had to pick up the car to change direction. Customer complaints forced the change to automatic reverse in 1935. This change required yet another casting adjustment, making the power car wider. Another addition in 1935 was the *Silver Streak Zephyr*, a five-car train that looked elegant sweeping around a wider 40-inch radius track.

Lionel, meanwhile, covered its bases by turning out a Zephyr clone, choosing to model the *Flying Yankee*, a short-line train operated by the Boston & Maine and Maine Central Railroad between Bangor, Maine, and Boston, Massachusetts.

To hedge their bets on the American Flyer Zephyr, lithographed versions were built out of sheet metal. Compared to

Lionel had put their money on the Union Pacific M-10000 to be the big seller for 1934, especially when the train won the race to be the first streamliner. While putting out various models of the M-10000, Lionel hedged its bets by building an O-Gauge model of the Boston & Maine and Maine Central Flying Yankee. It required Lionel's premium 72-inch-radius track (normal O-Gauge track has a 36-inch radius) and wore an odd two-tone paint job, but it was a shovelnose. Neither the M-10000 nor the Flying Yankee was a sale success, but all the models of the 1934 streamliners are valuable collectables today. (Gerry Souter Photo)

American Flyer toy electric trains spent 1933-1934 bird-dogging Budd Manufacturing and the CB&Q to get the plans of the 9900 Zephyr. They needed a model to be ready for the February Toy Fair in New York where the 1934 Christmas lines were revealed. The streamliner was a tough design to reproduce, but they managed with castings for the top-of-the-line and painted tin for the wind-up versions. (Courtesy, Barnes & Noble Publishing)

The American Flyer Zephyr that came out in O-Gauge was sold in this box to run on a regular three-rail track. Its articulation happened through pins in the roof. To reverse the original you had to pick up the power car to get at the reverse switch. The lower end models, both electric and wind-up, were not durable under real play conditions. In the end, the American Flyer Zephyr toy train was not a success. (Courtesy, Barnes & Noble Publishing)

When the American Flyer Christmas catalogs came out for 1934, gracing the cover was an illustration of the Pioneer Zephyr with "American Flyer Trains" as the nose art. The illustration was cropped from a painting commissioned by the CB&Q from artist O.E. Hake depicting spring, or rebirth, symbolically ushered in by Zephyrus, god of the West Wind. (Courtesy, Barnes & Noble Publishing)

the cast Zephyr price of $12, the sheet-metal electric-powered model with a lithographed silver and black exterior came off the dealer's shelf at $6. To squeeze the streamliner concept even further, American Flyer produced 800 series of wind-up, sheet-metal versions in three- and four- car configurations. All these sheet-metal trains used a thin grade of steel that didn't hold up to hard play. Many severely dented tin Zephyrs ended up in the trash can a short time after purchase. They are very rare today. A unique rooftop coupler pin was favored in the Flyer Zephyrs using hole tabs that extended above and below the roof shell with a linking pin held in place by gravity.

The 1327-RT model is modeled after "the (three unit) Twin Zephyrs, which speed from Chicago to the Twin Cities." The top model was the 1327-RCT *Silver Streak*, 52 inches long with a reversing motor and flicker-free lamps in the five units but without the actual articulation between cars, only simulating it with body decoration.[10]

Ultimately, neither American Flyer's Zephyr nor Lionel's M-10000 and *Flying Yankee* streamliners sold very well. Though they reflected the state of the art in prototype locomotive design, they and other steam-engine models that hid under "streamlined" shrouds in the mid- to late 1930s never looked right to consumers.

Dapper as usual, the Pioneer Zephyr driver wears his coverall, white shirt, and necktie as he throttles the four-car streamliner down the main and over the maze of tracks that weave through Council Bluffs, Iowa, just outside Omaha, Nebraska. Because of demand, a fourth car had to be added to the Zephyr's consist. The Zephyr's mail hook is latched down in the mail-room doorway and a close look reveals the sight glass in place used by the postal employee to spot the hanging mail bag at trackside while blasting along at 80 mph. (Denver Public Library, Otto Perry Collection)

Since the Zephyrs were articulated, they could only be turned using track laid out in a "Y" configuration. Called a "wye," the 9900 four-car train shown here uses the Cascade Wye near Burlington, Iowa when it stood in for the 9903 Mark Twain Zephyr on a run between St. Louis and Burlington. The CB&Q had to build wyes for each of its articulated trains, calling attention to that flaw in the streamliner's design. (Fred Kuepper Photo, Dave Lotz Collection)

Cocked and ready to go, the Zephyr rests on its track outside the machine shops at West Burlington. Preparing for the Denver-to-Chicago record run, employees volunteered to go over every inch of the silver streamliner with Bon Ami polish. Workers' families were invited to a company open house while spouses applied the elbow grease. Visible in the cab are two young ladies who are either shining up Jack Ford's office or getting a tour. (Dave Lotz Collection)

sea of felt fedora hats pressed in for a closer look as the NBC Radio Network set up for its remote broadcast. Big Sylvania Press No. 22 flashbulbs were screwed into Graphic Camera reflectors, and reporters listened for any unique quotes for the Enquirer's early Bulldog Edition. Albert Cotsworth's daughter, Marguerite, a student at Swarthmore College, had the honor of busting a champagne bottle over

the Zephyr's gleaming bow. As the bubbly splashed, an explosion of sirens, whistles, bells, and hoorahs filled the air. That accomplished, the first 24,000 potential passengers trooped through the train to stare and touch.

On April 18, the Zephyr made its official maiden run from Broad Street Station in Philadelphia to Paoli, Pennsylvania, a distance of a little under 25

miles, and back. They ran at night between eight and nine o'clock at a speed that hovered between 80 and 90 mph.

As the speed had climbed when the Zephyr's throttle advanced, so the CB&Q's marketing machinery rolled up into high revs as the train left Philadelphia to begin an exhibition tour of 30 cities in five weeks' time. Statistics were against Ralph Budd's railroad. Passenger revenues were dropping steadily and automobiles on the roads of the period between 1920 and 1930 had increased in numbers from 8 to 23 million cars. It was time to tie the whistle down once again.

The stainless-steel Zephyr proceeded on its tour to Detroit and then on to Cleveland, Pittsburgh, Cincinnati, Louisville, and Fort Wayne, Indiana. With its shovelnose pointed north toward Chicago, rolling on Pennsylvania Railroad tracks into a 40-mph headwind, the slippery silver Zephyr highballed across the Hoosier State. It rolled into Englewood Station on Chicago's south side with a timed run averaging 80 mph. The Eastern tour had introduced 380,000 visitors to the little train.

On May 11, from Englewood, the Zephyr clicked through the web of tracks that marked Chicago as the rail hub of the country and rolled onto a siding at the 1934 Century of Progress, then in its second year on the shore of Lake Michigan. Over the next two days

Otto Perry, train-photography hobbyist from the Denver area, caught the Pioneer Zephyr *slicing through Kansas on January 18, 1936. Note the sight glass angled out from the doorway of the Railway Post Office door. It's both larger and squarer than seen on later versions of the four-car* Pioneers. *(Denver Public Library, Otto Perry Photograph)*

In this sea of hats on April 17, 1934, are dignitaries from all over Philadelphia and the CB&Q front office to officially christen the new Zephyr, No. 9900, at the Broad Street train station. Both Budds were there as well as NBC radio for the occasion. The lady hunting for a place to bash her champagne bottle is Marguerite Cotsworth, daughter of the CB&Q passenger agent, Albert Cotsworth (BNSF Photo)

another 34,000 fairgoers wandered through the cars.

The silver train sat there like a sideshow on the midway. "See the bearded lady! See the world's largest ball of string! See the *Burlington Zephyr!*" The Zephyr was a novelty, a shiny toy with fits of speed built in, but would she bring passengers back to the CB&Q? Ralph Budd had considered that question as the Zephyr made its grand tour. Budd may have looked like an English professor, but he was a showman at heart. In Chicago he proposed an idea to the World's Fair Committee.

The *Burlington Zephyr* planned to head west to Denver and on May 26 begin a high-speed non-stop run to the Chicago World's Fair and arrive in time to re-open the second year of the fair at Edward Hungerford's history pageant, "Wings of a Century." The train had to start before dawn to arrive at dusk. The Chicago, Burlington & Quincy Railroad wanted an official world's record, held at the time by Britain's crack train, *The Royal Scot*. The Q's own steam-hauled pas-

America's First Diesel-Powered Streamlined Train

1 • Gleaming stainless steel strength members and outside surfaces assure solid long life and lasting beauty.

2 • Christened at Philadelphia on April 18, 1934, the *Pioneer Zephyr* #9900 starts on its road to fame.

3 • May 26, 1934. The *Pioneer Zephyr* leaves Denver for Chicago

on its history-making, record-breaking dawn to dusk run—averaging 77.6 miles per hour over more than 1,000 miles—with a top speed of 112.5.

4 • A star of the 1934 Chicago Century of Progress, the *Pioneer Zephyr* shares the limelight with Engine No. 35, a Burlington ancestor.

Using a series of photos, the CB&Q flaunts the original Zephyr's stainless-steel strength in its champagne christening in Philadelphia, poised in Denver to begin its race to Chicago on May 26, 1934, and on display at the Chicago Century of Progress Fairgrounds after its record-breaking dash. (Dave Lotz Collection)

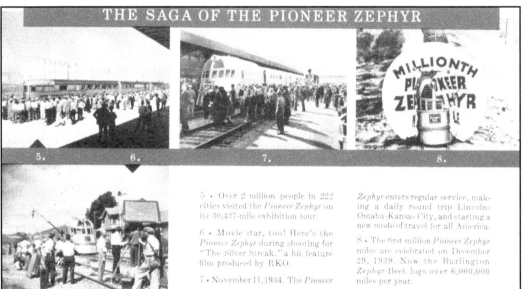

THE SAGA OF THE PIONEER ZEPHYR

5 • Over 2 million people in 222 cities visited the *Pioneer Zephyr* on its 30,437-mile exhibition tour.

6 • Movie star, too! Here's the *Pioneer Zephyr* during shooting for "The Silver Streak," a hit feature film produced by RKO.

7 • November 11, 1934. The *Pioneer*

Zephyr enters regular service, making a daily round trip Lincoln-Omaha-Kansas City, and starting a new mode of travel for all America.

8 • The first million *Pioneer Zephyr* miles are celebrated on December 29, 1939. Now the Burlington *Zephyr* fleet logs over 6,000,000 miles per year.

Hoopla and ballyhoo followed the Zephyrs wherever they went. The Pioneer Zephyr's PR army set the standard reviewed in this brochure. From clocking 30,437 miles of touring to starring as the Silver Streak in an RKO action movie, the Pioneer was rarely out of the public's mind. The shovelnose fleet managed to log over a million miles of service by December 1939. (Dave Lotz Collection)

9 • Winter and summer, the *Pioneer Zephyr* performs with round-the-clock efficiency. Here it slashes through a snowdrift at high speed.

10 • Guest of honor at its tenth birthday party, the *Pioneer Zephyr* cuts its own cake at Lincoln, Neb. on April 10, 1944.

11 • The *Pioneer Zephyr*, granddaddy of diesel-powered streamlined trains, at Quincy, Illinois celebrates its 20th anniversary of regular service.

12 • May 26, 1960. On permanent display at the Museum of Science and Industry, Chicago, Illinois.

The saga of the original Pioneer Zephyr celebrated in this brochure includes blasting through snowdrifts, celebrating birthdays, and standing alongside the next generation of Model E GM diesels. Finally, the Cinderella train was retired to Chicago's Museum of Science and Industry. Here, it would turn dingy and become a home for stray cats before its rebirth as an icon of successful functional design. (Dave Lotz Collection)

On its westward tour following the record-breaking run, the 9900 Zephyr stopped at all the significant railroad engineering feats such as the Dotsero Cutoff and Moffat Tunnel where it emerged and backed until all the waiting press had their photos. (BNSF Photo)

A rare photo shows the buffet grill aboard the 9900 Zephyr actually inhabited by a smiling steward. Behind and above him is the Stromberg Carlson 11-tube radio that was responsible for entertainment piped into the three cars through brass-grilled speakers. Tuning the radio was the steward's responsibility. If you didn't want to miss an episode of Ma Perkins, you tipped well. Also visible are the coffee urns and the grill hotplate for sandwiches. Across the front is a lino-covered serving counter. (BNSF Photo)

Unique nose art adorns the 9900 Zephyr for its movie debut as the hero in a B action movie titled Silver Streak that came out in 1934. The streamliner was the only train capable of delivering an iron lung to an injured worker at Hoover Dam. A hair-raising rush from Chicago to the dam site (not unlike the Zephyr's record-breaking speed run) with Hollywood near-misses delivered the lung and redeemed the futuristic train everyone had put down as "impractical" and a waste of money. (BNSF Photo)

senger flyer, *The Aristocrat*, required 26 hours to cover the same distance – with a total of 40 stops, of course – but still, there were a lot of scoffs and not a few crossed fingers among CB&Q employees when the challenge was accepted.

This story has been told many times by excellent writers, some with personal experience of the event, but we have to tell it here again if only to show how all the parts and technologies, how all the contributions from more than 100 vendors came together to create one of the great legendary runs in the history of railroading.

Following the explosion of publicity, the 9900 *Burlington Zephyr* settled into being a showpiece again at the fair. Endless lines of visitors trooped through the

The *Burlington Zephyr's* Record-Breaking Run

The Mile-High City's Union Station was busy on the overcast morning of May 26, 1934, and a surprising number of railroad officials, city officials, celebrities, and rubbernecks were on hand to witness a world-record speed attempt. It was 5:00 A.M. Denver time, and everyone who was supposed to be on board the waiting *Burlington Zephyr* train had taken their seats or crowded into the cab next to Jack Ford, the engineer who would rotate shifts at the throttle with Ernie Weber and Ernie Kuehne. Both Ralph Budd and Ed Budd were there along with practically the entire CB&Q front office, just arrived from Philadelphia. Enough press crowded in to make sure not a single pithy quote went unrecorded, nor a single liquor bottle unsampled. For that time in the morning, it was a mostly happy crowd that watched the hands of the wooden timing clock for the instant the timing tape tethered to the Zephyr was released as the great adventure began. At least that was the impression.

They were an hour late and those who knew the truth of the situation were somewhat more subdued. Twelve hours earlier, technicians had discovered a busted armature bearing in one of the two GE model T16 traction motors. Not wanting to tip off the press or the assembling crowd of dignitaries, Ralph Budd and his team began quietly hunting about for a replacement. Their efforts turned up a bearing, but it was days away in Detroit. One of the team members made a crack about how the Union Pacific would love to make public how the great *Burlington Zephyr* was stalled in Denver for want of a bearing.

Ralph Budd picked up the telephone. He knew what other high-speed train had a similar pair of GE self-ventilated T-16 traction motors. Against the apoplectic pleadings of his publicity people, Budd called Carl Gray, president of the Union Pacific Railroad, and asked if Carl's people had a spare bearing of the kind used on their M-10000's traction motors. Gray said he had one. A mechanic would be on the first plane from Omaha to Cheyenne with the part. A chartered plane would take him to Denver by 12:30 A.M. Ralph made sure the Burlington's assistant vice president, Fred Gurley, would be ready to meet the plane with a police escort to bring the bearing to the Zephyr.

As the wait went on amid the pacing and muttering, Burlington vice president Ed Flynn answered the phone. On the other end was the editor of the Rocky Mountain News asking if the Zephyr could squeeze in one more passenger

With bands playing, spotlights washing over its gleaming stainless surface, and ringed by applauding crowds, the 9900 breaks the world speed record in its run from Denver to Chicago on May 26,1934. Outside, there's the World's Fair Hall of Transportation stage. Inside, a crush of dignitaries prepares to meet the press – sprucing up their breath with Sen-Sen. Also inside is Zeph the Colorado burro – his stomach swelled with breakfast food to forestall the effects of motion sickness – and a lot of wrinkled riders who've never traveled so fast in their lives. (BNSF Photo)

headed for Colorado's exhibit at the World's Fair. It was a "Rocky Mountain Canary" named Zeph and all he'd need was some hay for one end and straw for the other. Zeph was a small pack burro of the kind used by Colorado gold miners and would reside in the baggage compartment for the duration of the trip and then take up residence at Colorado's fairground pavilion. Ralph Budd's classic reply to Flynn's query has remained a fixture in railroad lore.

"Why not? One more jackass on this trip won't make any difference."

As the bearing was being installed, the Burlington's publicity people continued to spoon down the Bromo Seltzer as they contemplated the Union Pacific's PR coup announcing how they saved the CB&Q from embarrassment. Again Budd stepped in. He suggested the Q break the story as a courtesy to the UP and to show how rivals could pull together when a world record was at stake.

At 5:04 A.M., while mechanics wiped grease off their hands, Jack Ford released the brakes and eased the throttle forward on its quadrant. A gentleman wearing a neat gray suit and a straw fedora on his head whipped down a green flag once used to start the Indianapolis 500 Race. The timing tape snapped free and the official Western Union clock began its measurement. Down the track, 1,017.6 miles away, waited the Transportation Building at the Chicago World's Fair. How long the wait would be was anybody's guess.

For a while, it seemed that the speed record might also be in jeopardy as the Zephyr poked along at 50 mph. Burlington mechanics and Budd engineers had insisted on the slow speed to ease the new bearing into operation. A bit at a time, apprehension eased as Ford felt the big diesel at his back begin to take the strain and 78 miles out from Denver the town of Fort Morgan, Colorado, flashed past at the 68-minute mark. The chatter of pistons blended into a feral roar as the speed gauge settled on 90 mph for 129 miles. Through the shovelnose cab windows, individual ties became a single blurred ribbon between the rails for almost 20 miles while the needle edged past 106 mph. At 109 no one in the crowded cab spoke. Some VIPs nervously left the confined cab space as trains waiting on sidings hurtled past in a freakish flash of colors and indistinct shapes, hurling back the howl of the Zephyr's wheels on steel. Lips were dry and eyes were large when the speedometer touched 112.5 mph.

Back in the coaches and observation solarium, the mood was festive and only a few eyebrows were raised as the Zephyr's speed at one point dipped down from its blazing rush. Up front all was chaos. One of the reporters, who had made extra sure the gin was of fine quality, had gone forward to watch the cab action. Feeling the draft blown back by the fans behind the two big front-end grilles, he slammed the steel door shut to the mailroom. This helpful gesture severed a makeshift cable and produced a hot-flash short circuit, which caused engineer Ernie Kuehne to shut down the engine. Without the cable the engine could not be restarted. Revs began to drop. The Zephyr rolled on down a grade without power for 34 miles. Burlington assistant chief engineer Roy Baer worked with others to try and splice the severed cable but had no luck. The Zephyr still had the grade working for it, but its speed had dropped to 40 mph. Finally, in desperation, Baer took both ends of the cable in his hands and advised Kuehne to hit the starter. The engineer did just that as Baer pressed the raw wires together. The big hot diesel engine jumped, blew out a burp of exhaust, and caught. For an instant, Roy Baer became part of the electrical circuit, long enough to cook both his hands. The engine restarted as Baer was led to the rear to find what first aid was available for his third-degree burns.

The world's record run was made possible by an army of helpers, many of whom manned the 1,070 public grade crossings that required two flagmen to stop traffic, or the 619 private crossings where one man stood guard. Every switch was spiked open to the main an hour before the Zephyr's arrival. All trains, freight and passenger, were shunted onto sidings. One result of this attention to detail was an unexpected side effect. Constant running and blowing the Zephyr's air horn at junctions depleted its air reservoirs. When the reservoirs reached an established low point, automatic sensors were designed to close the Westinghouse air brakes, effectively stopping the train. Knowing this, Ernie Kuehne goosed the throttle and watched the dial needles

snap to the right. As the diesel engine revs suddenly rose, the compressors kicked in and the reservoirs began refilling. With the sun sinking at its back, reflecting hot copper off stainless steel, the Zephyr continued to scorch the rails in its determined non-stop rush through 164 cities and past the admiring gaze of a half-million Depression-weary Americans toward Chicago.

Bands played, signs were displayed, and dignitaries clustered in small groupings for the press photographers' flashbulbs as the Zephyr posed on the *Wings of the Century* stage with the stygian dark of Lake Michigan at its back. Breaking the second timing tape and the world's record at the Chicago end of the run had taken 13 hours, 4 minutes and 58 seconds at an average speed of 77.61 mph. The run had used up 418 gallons of diesel fuel from the 600-gallon tank, producing 2.43 miles per gallon. Total cost in fuel to move 197,000 lbs of train 1,117.6 miles at speeds up to 112 mph was four cents a gallon or $16.72. No steam train could have accomplished such economy and efficiency.

From the moment the *Burlington Zephyr* rolled into Chicago on its way to the World's Fair Transportation Building on May 26, 1934, diesel-electric locomotion became confirmed as the ascendant form of motive power in American rail transportation.

With the Goodyear Tires blimp cruising overhead, a long, long line winds its way past the Burlington Route's lakefront exhibit at Chicago's World's Fair in its second year, 1934. Dressed in their Sunday best, people pass up the shiny new Hudson steam engine, the little historic 4-4-0 American locomotive with its quaint diamond stack and toy-like cars, to peer at and file into the famous Zephyr that shattered a world's speed record and just looks like something out of a Flash Gordon comic book. (BNSF Photo)

now world-famous cars. They saw where Zeph the burro had ridden in his crate in the baggage car. They heard how he'd become sick and dined on breakfast food from the buffet until his digestive crisis passed. They saw where Wayne Wigdon shared the baggage space with the sick burro and where the burro crate had fallen on him while the train rounded a tight curve at 100 mph. Additional passengers occupying 10 extra chairs in the baggage compartment had hauled the crate off the boy and his equipment.

Wigdon had gamely tapped away on his Morse key, alerting station agents and the press to the Zephyr's location and speed during the run. There were no portable telephones or wireless mobile radios at that time, so 17-year-old Wigdon, the son of a Burlington employee, had been allowed to set up a small table with his Morse equipment. The equip-

ment connected to three antennas welded to the roof of the train, each 12 inches high and separated by 22 feet. The receiver for his messages was at his home in Aurora, Illinois, and was manned by two trusted friends. His transmission lines then connected to the Burlington Depot and the office of the Aurora dispatcher who distributed Wayne's reports along the route. All the more remarkable to the World's Fair visitors was learning that Wayne had figured out the entire installation himself and had been a radio operator for six years, having received his HAM radio license at age 11.

Wayne Wigdon received 52 cents an hour for the trip and went on to become Communications Director for the Burlington Northern Railroad. He retired in 1977.[11]

After a short tour of duty at the fair, the Zephyr slipped out again and headed

West to spread the word. Everywhere it went, Burlington PR photographers posed the Zephyr against breathtaking backdrops of western scenery. The silver train participated in opening the Dotsero Cutoff, a 38-mile stretch of track that linked two railroads with the Moffat Tunnel, which ran for 6.2 miles under the Continental Divide, shortening the route between Denver and Salt Lake City, Utah, by 173 miles. The Zephyr went on to tour the West Coast, pose with the M-10000, and finally head back to Chicago via the Royal Gorge in mid-July. Once again installed at the fair, another 709,000 visitors passed through its cars before the Zephyr made a test run between the Twin Cities (Minneapolis and St. Paul, Minnesota) and Chicago. It covered the distance in six hours at an average speed of 71 mph. This market seemed ready-made for a Zephyr… or maybe two.

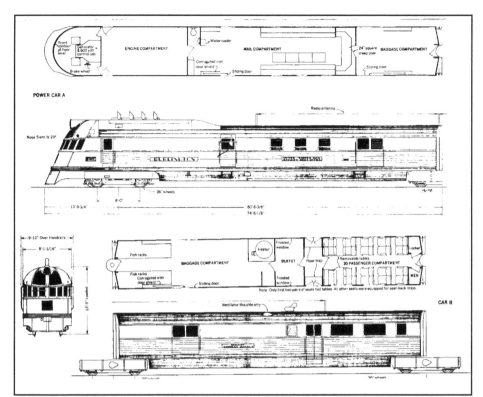

Exterior and interior diagrams of the 1934 Burlington Zephyr before it became the Pioneer. With everything else in its proper place, a long radio antenna sits atop the roof of the power car and the first passenger car. The antenna never appeared in revenue service but was affixed during the record-breaking run from Denver to Chicago by the 17-year-old telegrapher Wayne Wigdon. (Courtesy, Flying Yankee Restoration Group)

Eventually, the 9900 Zephyr was named the *Pioneer Zephyr* and introduced with a round of excursions for future riders. On November 11, 1934, the new train (actually trains 20 and 21 on the schedule) was put into service leaving Lincoln, Nebraska, in the morning and traveling to Kansas City by way of Omaha. Building revenue at first on curiosity riders and then adding commuters from there, the schedule's ridership continued to climb until increases of 96 percent, 128 percent, and 160 percent were achieved. Even the two remaining steam-powered trains increased their passenger loads. Passenger miles climbed for the Burlington by 26 percent between December 1934 and January 1935 over the same two-month

This photo from the Burlington Northern Santa Fe Archive shows the 9900 Zephyr passing through Aurora, Illinois, on its way to the Chicago World's Fair on its record run in May 1934. Closer inspection shows the photo was retouched to remove Wayne Wigdon's radio antenna, which was strung along the train's three roofs. (BNSF Photo)

Looking dapper, the official starter confers with Winton engineer Ernie Kuehn three minutes (according to the timing clock at left) before the 9900 Zephyr begins its dawn-to-dusk attempt to break the world speed record on its way to the Chicago World's Fair. A strand of tape is stretched tight between the clock and the locomotive. The onlookers on the platform are taut. Inside the cab, it's standing room only, but everyone is relaxed because the gin was uncapped an hour ago – the time it took to replace a bad bearing with a new one on loan from the Union Pacific Railroad. (BNSF Photo)

Parked in front of the magnificent CB&Q train station in Burlington, Iowa, the new 9900 Zephyr drew daily crowds prior to its inauguration. Summer dresses and straw hats adorn this June 1934 crowd as they pore over the revolutionary train before it begins revenue service. (Dave Lotz Collection)

period the previous years. The front office was amazed and managed only one complaint.

The press of reservations quickly loaded up every run and the 72 seats designated for passengers weren't enough. On June 24, 1935, an additional 40-seat articulated passenger coach was spliced into the train in front of the parlor car, where it remained for the remainder of its service life, some 28 years.

The phenomenal little train had boosted passenger traffic between its three cities by at least 150 percent. Ticket sellers discovered people were willing to stand during a Zephyr ride rather than sit aboard a steam-hauled train.

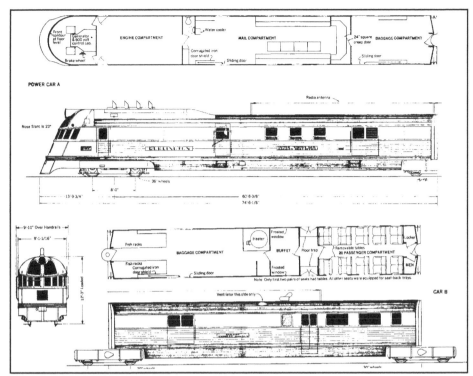

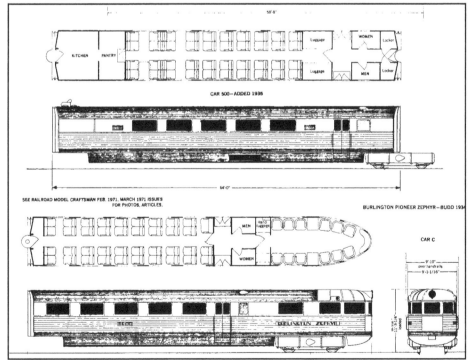

This diagram of the Pioneer Zephyr is unique in that it includes the radio antenna rigged for the cross-country record run in 1934 and a second seat in the operator's compartment. A radio antenna appeared on subsequent models of the Pioneer Zephyr, but the masts are considerably shorter and are confined to the roof of the mail/baggage car. (Courtesy, Railroad Model Craftsman Magazine)

These illustrations show the Pioneer Zephyr after it received its extra car, No. 500, in 1935, added on to meet riders' needs due to the huge popularity of the train. The car holds an additional 40 passengers plus a pantry and a kitchen to supplement the buffet grill. (Courtesy, Railroad Model Craftsman Magazine)

The plated alloy coin was minted in 1984 to commemorate 50 years since the Pioneer Zephyr made its record run to the 1934 World of Progress Fair in Chicago. The fair opened in 1933 at the height of the Great Depression. The arrival of the "First Diesel Streamliner" at the Transportation Building after the train's famous speed trial was a highlight of the fair's second year. Also depicted are the Transportation Building and the searchlight beams that lit up Chicago's lakefront each night. (Courtesy, Flying Yankee Restoration Group, Gerry Souter Photo)

The sky is still bright as the 9900 Zephyr rushes through Aurora, Illinois, toward its date with history. This is near the end of the famous dawn-to-dusk record-breaking run from Denver to Chicago on May 26, 1934. The little three-car train was new technology scorching the rails into Depression-era Chicago and its place on the stage of the World's Fair. Note Wayne Wigdon's two-way radio antenna mast on the car roofs. Wigdon rigged the transmitter-receiver himself to broadcast the Zephyr's progress. His broadcast "booth" was a small table in the baggage car next to Zeph the Burro. (L. E. Griffith Photo, Jim Singer Collection)

CHAPTER FOUR

TWIN ZEPHYRS 9901– 9902 CREATE A "FLEET"

A rarely seen sight once revenue service began, but there was always time for another PR shot. Here, the 9901 and 9902 Twin Cities Zephyrs line up near Aurora, Illinois. The next day, both trains, with special permission, ran side-by-side from Aurora to Chicago for their christening. (BNSF Photo)

Following test runs, to handle what was perceived to be a very lucrative market between Minnesota's Twin Cities and the city of Chicago, the Burlington requested Budd Manufacturing to assemble not one, but two more Zephyrs virtually identical to the three-car *Pioneer* – the *Twin Zephyrs*, Nos. 9901 and 9902. These identical streamliners had their fuel capacity increased from 600 to 660 gallons and the power car was seven feet shorter than the *Pioneer*, due to the loss of the Railway Post Office contract. Also, the two grille covers on the head end no longer frowned at the world with a downward tilt. The horn had been moved from behind the air intake grilles to the top of the roof, and a second seat for a crewman was added to the operator's compartment. This last change answered a criticism among railroad men that grew over the next five years concerning the safety of the stylish shovelnose design. It also reflected the strong railroad unions' constant worry about loss of jobs.

The Brotherhood of Locomotive Firemen and Enginemen had complained that operating the Zephyr with just one man was unsafe. The CB&Q claimed the dead-man button on the air brake and foot pedal that stopped the train if released overcame that objection. Ultimately, however, the second crewman was added. Later, when "B" units containing additional diesel power plants were mandated so longer trains could be hauled, railroad management fought against adding a complete second crew to the "cabless" engine cars by not painting an identifying number on those units, making them an "extension" of the head-end power car. The diesel engines built by Electro-Motive were also linked so they were dependent on each other. Both were operated solely by the crew in the head-end cab.

To Budd's and the CB&Q's credit, with each iteration of the Zephyr concept they improved on the original. The *Pioneer Zephyr* turned out to be a rolling test laboratory that begat a small but successful fleet of trains, each more stylish and efficient than its predecessor, and at least as popular. The Q's publicity department was sodden with the success of the first *Pioneer Zephyr*, and was desperate to keep the waves of headlines and public acceptance rolling in. As soon as the 9901 *Twin Zephyr* was tagged fit for service and pushed out the Budd shop door on March 23, a load of 88 passengers was bundled aboard and

One of the 1935 three-car Twin Zephyrs *hurries along the track paralleling the Mississippi River. The pair of Zephyrs caused a lot of stir with the traveling public, resulting in fully booked trips between Chicago and Minneapolis. (BNSF Photo)*

After rolling into Chicago after a trip running side by side from Aurora, Illinois, on April 15, 1935, the 9901 and 9902 Twin Cities Zephyrs disgorged a collection of human twins, herded together by the ever-clever CB&Q PR department. Here, twin sisters Marion and Francis Beeler stand poised with the unsettling group of identicals, ready to swat the locomotives with bottles of bubbly. (BNSF Photo)

sent rushing over Seaboard Air Line Railroad track through the south to Florida. Along the way, folks in big cities and small towns such as Washington, Richmond, Columbia, Jacksonville, Ocala, West Palm Beach, Tampa, St. Petersburg, and Sarasota made a fuss over its arrival. By the time the 9901 had traveled 2,861 miles, more than 136,000 persons had trooped aboard.

For this spectacular eyeball run, the CB&Q shelled out $43.72 in fuel cost. The *Twin Zephyr* returned on April 2, 1935, just as newspaper headlines were starting to wrap fish and line birdcages. On April 6 the same three-car train set off for Chicago loaded with railroad front-office brass. The 9901 *Twin Zephyr* scorched the tracks to Chicago in five hours and 33 minutes. While averaging around 77 mph, on one straight stretch of track the streamliner hit a top speed of 104. Under flinty-eyed scrutiny, 9901 turned around and rushed back to St. Paul. When the dipsticks were examined, round trip statistics showed 2.6 miles per gallon of diesel oil burned and two gallons of lubricating oil consumed.

For the next week, the train traveled all over Burlington country, up and down the right of way, transporting city fathers, chambers of commerce, and anyone else who had a cleaned and pressed suit. Finally arriving in Aurora, Illinois, on April 14, the 9901 braked to a stop next to its sister Zephyr, the 9902, which had arrived the day before. The PR department had collected 44 sets of identical twins of all ages and genders dressed in their Sunday best. With cameras grinding and flashbulbs popping, these matching sets rode the pair of Zephyrs, gliding along side by side on the three-track main line, to Chicago. More hoopla ensued, champagne flowed, speeches rung the rafters of Union Station, and the collection of dignitaries hurried off to St. Paul for a special luncheon. By April 20, everyone was pretty much partied out and the *Twin Zephyrs* were put into their regular scheduled service starting the next day.

While the external *Twins* appeared virtually identical to the *Pioneer*, the internal alterations were considerable. With the loss of the Railway Post Office contract, more baggage space was available in the 66-foot power car. There was also room to expand the kitchen facilities. The buffet on the 9900 had been adequate for that train's short run, but a full kitchen equipped for a 10-hour trip's worth of food and beverage service was needed for the *Twins*. At the back of the baggage section in the power car, a kitchen annex with a large sink for the pearl diver (dishwasher) was located across from the steam generator, and storage lockers were built above the battery compartment. The fish racks, wood floor mats used in the baggage compartment to keep wet floors from becoming slippery, were extended past the vestibule into this larger kitchen area.

Facing into the second car, the fully electrified kitchen was fitted out to create complete meals, compared to the sandwiches and light fare offered by the *Twins'* grill. An electric range, heated steam table, warming closet, and refrigerator were supplemented with iceboxes and chests for crushed ice and a large four-unit coffee urn. The previous buffet space now served as a pantry with iceboxes and built-ins to store ice cream and dairy products. The original Formica workspace was turned into a dining

The 9901 leaves a station and picks up speed through a crossing on a two-line main paralleling a long passing siding. Hundreds of small-grade crossings kept the Zephyr from realizing its full high-speed potential once in service. The flat Midwestern landscape, however, did allow spurts of speed that thrilled passengers and train watchers alike. (BNSF Photo)

Twins Give Birth to an Automobile

In 1935 the Lincoln Motor Company had not yet been absorbed into Ford and was looking for a name to affix to its latest offering in the mid-price range. The car was a big 122-inch-wheelbase sedan with smooth contours and headlights streamlined into the fenders, powered by a huge V-12 engine developing 110 hp. It was heavy with steel girder reinforcement and boasted an honest (at two bits a gallon) "...14 to 18 miles per gallon of gas!" The newspapers were full of the CB&Q's famous record-breaking Zephyr trains. Choosing to tag onto this overnight fame, Lincoln sales manager Arthur S. "Hardrock" Hatch offered up the name "Lincoln Zephyr" and the name stuck. Offered as the new 1936 model, the Lincoln Zephyr remained on the market until 1942 brought an end to virtually all nonwar-related new car production. (Prepared with the help of the Lincoln Zephyr Owners Club, www.lzoc.org)

A shiny new Lincoln Zephyr automobile parked next to the 9902 Twin Zephyr at Chicago's Union Station. The engineer of the Twin Zephyr, Mr. Jim Kurns, has his foot on the car's bumper. Compared to many of the late 1930s car designs, the Zephyr featured headlights sculpted into the fenders, a sleek look, and a huge power plant under the hood. It was much more sellable than the magnificent flop, the Chrysler Airflow, which was of the same vintage. (Courtesy, Lincoln Zephyr Owners Club)

In 1939, the Lincoln Motor Company featured a new model based on the sculpted, streamlined concept of the Burlington Zephyr. The Lincoln Zephyr offered a V-12 engine delivering 110 hp and put out an honest "14 to 18 miles per gallon." Of course, in 1939 gas was 10 cents a gallon. Lincoln always showed the two Zephyrs together and, of course, Burlington was delighted. The car went away at the start of World War II, as did all new cars, and did not return. (Courtesy, Lincoln Zephyr Owners Club)

counter with four stools for passengers. The balance of the 58-foot, 8-inch second car offered 16 passengers a dinette section with fold-away black Formica tables. It also carried individual reclining seats in pairs for 40 passengers plus racks for hand baggage and separate washroom facilities for men and women.

Passing through to the 69-foot, 6-inch third car of the original three-car design, passengers followed the 20-inch-wide aisle past handbag storage and recliner seating for 24 riders. Bulkheads behind the last row of seating separated the cabin from the entry-exit vestibule and men's and women's washrooms.

The primary feature of the third car was the 24-seat parlor compartment, dou-

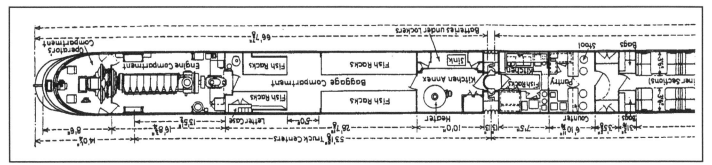

The layout of the Twin Zephyrs shows the Zephyr concept was flexible, adapting to individual route needs. For safety's sake, a fireman's seat has been added to the cab, nonslip fish-rack flooring has been added to the baggage space, and the steam generator for heating is now in the power car allowing room for a "pearl diver" sink and an enlarged kitchen facility and pantry for the grill. Stools for counter seating have also been added to the front of the 20-seat passenger space. (Courtesy Railway Age)

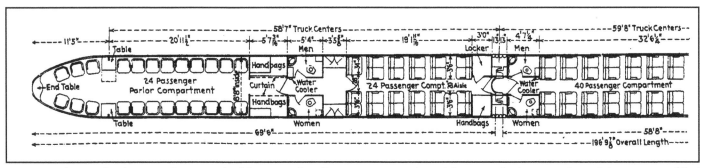

Passenger heavy, the three-car Twins packed them into the 40-passenger coach and then into the last car where 24 passengers filled out the parallel seating before a door and a curtain parted for admittance into the parlor-observation car. Arrayed around the walls to the round end with the curious little table, individual chairs faced each other like two 12-member teams waiting for the game to begin. The intimacy of the Pioneer's parlor car was gone, turning the "first class" accommodation into a doctor's waiting room with moving scenery. (Courtesy, Railway Age)

ble the capacity of the original *Pioneer*. Enunciator buttons connected this observation lounge with the kitchen for beverage service and three tables were built in along with ashtrays in weighted-base stands. The parlor car seats in the *Twins* were more comfortable than the straight-back seats furnished with the first parlor car concept. One and a quarter inches were trimmed off the rear legs of each chair so it naturally reclined. Later that same year, specs for the *Mark Twain Zephyr* specified the arm rests be lowered 1/2-inch, and that adjustment also was transferred to the *Twin Zephyrs*.

One other lesson learned from the *Pioneer* was improved access to hand baggage in the passenger compartments. Originally, the seats were built high enough off the floor so handbags slid beneath. But in the 9901 and 9902 *Twin Zephyrs* and subsequent models, over-

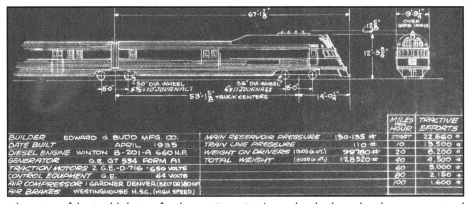

Blueprints of the Budd design for the two Twin Zephyrs clearly show the changes required from the original Pioneer. The Twins' power cars had seven feet lopped off due to the lack of the Railway Post Office. The rake of the roof becomes steeper and entry to the cab is closer to the front, forcing the number board from the lower side to above the doorway. The Twin also has only a single double-door to the baggage space. The "frown" face of the power car's head end is gone completely as commonsense standardization of window sizes replaced fanciful concepts. (Burlington Route Historical Society)

head racks were added. As the 9900 was shifted around to other routes, overhead luggage racks were retrofitted. While

Zephyr routes increased in length and demand kept pace, the interior amenities were continually upgraded.

Twin Zephyrs rushed along their route between Minneapolis and Chicago in tandem as part of a photo op and to let folks waiting at stations along the route know the new service was about to begin. The PR campaign was so successful that in a short time after inauguration of the two-train schedule, the little three-car streamliners were hopelessly overcrowded. (Burlington Route Historical Society)

Perfect placement of the camera for this dramatic shot tips the hand of the CB&Q public relations flacks and a busy crew armed with snow shovels to create the "snowbank." They had the Zephyrs busting through snow, paper hoops, and anything else that would generate free ink in the popular press. (Burlington Route Historical Society)

Since the *Twin Zephyrs* followed the Mississippi River down to Chicago, the cool-to-neutral paint scheme used in the *Pioneer* made sense, complementing the changing moods of the meandering river. The Masonite panels were sized, joined with waterproof cement, sanded, and then primed with Dolfinite Red Metal Primer. The paint was designated as "eggshell gloss enamel," a proprietary form of semi-gloss. The color scheme used by the Dolphin Paint and Varnish Company consisted of Dolfinite:

Eggshell Gloss White
Eggshell Gloss Cream
Eggshell Gloss Gray-Green
Eggshell Gloss Blue-Gray
Eggshell Gloss Buff
Eggshell Gloss Kitchen Green

Mechanically, there were also improvements to the trains' amenities and operations. Double hermetical sealing of the windows improved effectiveness of the air conditioning and helped further deaden outside sound. Windows were made of two 1/4-inch pieces of Duplate™ glass (plate glass panels sandwiching thin plastic sheet) used on Chrysler-Plymouth autos. An air space was left between the panels to prevent fogging and misting.

Once again, a Peter Smith boiler fired from an oil tank provided steam heat at the rate of 500 lbs per hour to radiators in each car. Automatic thermostats placed near the floor of each car regulated that car's heat while air-conditioning thermostats were placed halfway up each wall to maintain a comfort balance.

Air-compressor efficiency was improved by replacing the two motor-operated compressors used on the *Pioneer Zephyr* to provide 25 cubic feet of air per minute with a single Gardner-Denver 75-cubic-foot compressor. Air braking came from a new Westinghouse HSC system developed for high-speed articulated train applications. An electrically activated pneumatic brake clamped down uniformly on the articulated truck wheels, shaving a split second off the activation time. If all electric power failed, a straight air-brake system was still available to halt the train. As with many of these improvements, the new brakes were also retrofitted to the 9900 *Pioneer*.

Competition over the Twin Cities route to Chicago heated up considerably with the pair of Zephyrs zooming back and forth with an admirable record of 97 percent availability. Both the Milwaukee Road's steam-powered *Hiawatha* and the Chicago and Northwestern's 400 Class steamers added sections to their premier runs. Curiously, the pair of Zephyrs had such drawing power and struggled with limited seating capacity to meet demand that the CB&Q was forced to order up steam-train sections for patrons, and those steamer-served schedules prospered as well, considerably increasing the Burlington's market share on that busy route.

The *Pioneer Zephyr* began racking up new revenue at a great rate and the *Twins* were poised to perform the same job. The front office went along with the flow, and in March 1935, just before the *Twins* were delivered, they ordered up another shovelnose from Budd. The 442-mile daily round trip route between St. Louis, Missouri, and Burlington, Iowa, had become a drag on the purse strings. This fourth version of the Zephyr line would put a stop to that.

CHAPTER FIVE

THE *MARK TWAIN ZEPHYR* 9903

The 92-seat Mark Twain Zephyr rolls through Burlington, Iowa, heading for its service run between that city and St. Louis with a stop at Twain's hometown of Hannibal, Missouri. The Becky Thatcher followed Injun Joe *with lunch on the burner in* Huckleberry Finn *and* Tom Sawyer *bringing up the rear. (Burlington Route Historical Society)*

This next variation on the design concept was also the first Zephyr train set to have a theme. It was named the *Mark Twain Zephyr*, No. 9903. Its route traversed what was perceived to be "Mark Twain Country," with a stop at the famous writer's hometown of Hannibal, Missouri. This train was something the CB&Q's public-relations battalion could get its teeth into. Carrying the burden of the American Bard's name, it was also designed as a longer and more powerful Zephyr coming out of the shop rather than depending upon retrofits.

Not content with just appropriating the author's name, the CB&Q named each one of the train's four cars. One can almost visualize the glee in the boardroom as Twain's creations were bandied about, searching for the best fits. The power car leading the literary band received the very nonpolitically correct appellation of *Injun Joe* – a play on words around "engine." This unit carried the usual head-end motive power, 30 feet worth of railway mail sorting space, and a 15-foot mail storage allotment.

Second in line, dubbed the *Becky Thatcher*, No. 506 was one long 64-foot baggage car. Trailing the luggage came No. 551, the *Huckleberry Finn*. This car offered a complete, though miniaturized, kitchen connected to a 16-seat dining section that led to 20 reclining coach seats in pairs. Dining service was extended to passengers in seats through the use of aluminum trays supported by two skeletonized supports that slid into slots on the back of the seat in front of the passenger. The result was a cantilevered tray not unlike today's airliner seat configurations. These trays could also be requested for card playing or paperwork to be accomplished *en route*. The convenience of foot

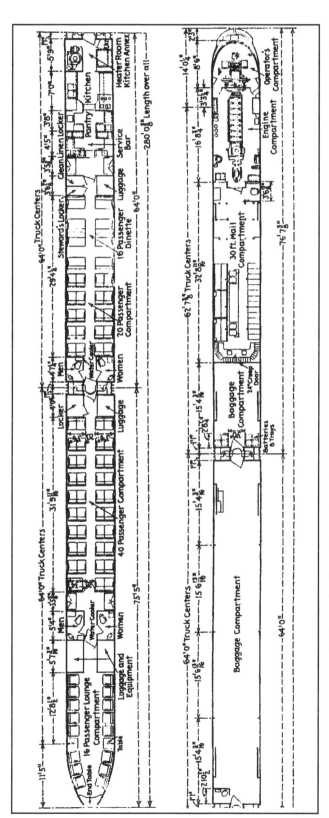

Always ready to learn, Budd and the Burlington created the Mark Twain Zephyr as a four-car unit with extra passenger capacity from the outset. Here, the power car more closely resembles the Pioneer Zephyr *due to the railway post office space behind the engine compartment and the baggage space entered through the small "creep door" beneath the mail-sorting bench. Also note the five trays of batteries added to the baggage space. Budd frequently juggled operating systems throughout the compartments, trying different combinations. The second car is one big baggage storage, requiring the steam generator be stuffed into the kitchen-pantry area behind the grill. Added is a 16-passenger dinette to the 20-passenger smoking section. The parlor lounge added four more chairs to its first-class space. (Courtesy,* Railway Age*)*

With its polished shovelnose parked in the Burlington, Iowa, depot, The Mark Twain 9903 takes on passengers and baggage for the run to St. Louis. Note the baggage cart disgorging a load into the baggage space behind the Twain's mail room leans dangerously close to stainless-scraping disaster as it tries to get as close as possible to the door. (Burlington Route Historical Society)

rails and overhead hand baggage racks and men's/women's lavatories was also standard equipment.

Following *Huckleberry* came *Tom Sawyer*, No. 572, the combination chair and parlor car. Here, a 40-chair passenger section abutted a 16-seat parlor/observation car. Another set of lavatories and hand-luggage storage separated the two compartments. Seating 92 passengers, the four-car combination stretched out about 280 feet and weighed 287,000 lbs. The very last element to hurry past a trackside bystander was a bronze relief right profile of Twain above his signature scribed in stainless steel and bolted to *Tom Sawyer's* backside. Twain might have enjoyed the irony.

For power demands, the standard 600-hp diesel electric Winton 201A engine still rested on its hardened steel bed poking up into the operators' compartment and sharing the power car with the Railway Post Office. The space for baggage was only a huge empty box with one small toilet for the crew. Located in the kitchen-pantry complex in *Huckleberry Finn* was the steam heater for the train. Here, the former Peter Smith boiler was replaced

Blueprints show the Mark Twain *was a ringer for the* Pioneer *as far as windows and doors were concerned, but kept the cab door forward as on the* Twins *and added the power car's name,* Injun Joe – *a play on the word "engine" – on its side. Also, dual horns were mounted on the roof. (Burlington Route Historical Society)*

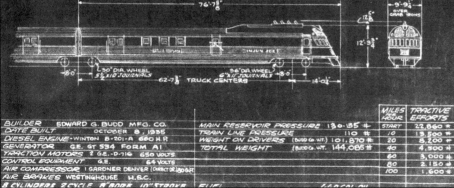

The Cascade Wye outside Burlington, Iowa, was a popular place for photographers to hang out when seeking Zephyrs. Here, the Mark Twain *eases back toward the main line from being turned around on the Y-shaped track. Like the* Pioneer *and the* Twins, *the* Twain *had to be turned as a unit. (Frank Kuepper photo, Dave Lotz Collection)*

with a Clarkson coil-type device also provided by the Vapor Car Heating Company of Chicago.

Frigidare supplied the air conditioning to all passenger compartments through mechanical equipment in the floors and ceilings of each car. Electrical systems were battery-powered, charged by a 220-volt, 60-cycle A.C. motor that drove a compressor in the D.C. motor, which, in turn, became a generator and charged the batteries. Also available was a belt-driven GT1177A-1 auxiliary generator and three CP-127B-11 motor-driven air compressors. The diesel engine operated the huge GT-534 main generator that powered the two GE 716 traction motors attached to the front power truck.

The trucks themselves continued to be housed in articulated modules, eliminating 34 wheels from a conventional passenger car consist and those wheels' attendant friction. Outside-type Timken

Once it was decided that the Denver to Chicago route would be a good idea, while two new Zephyrs were being built, both the Pioneer *and the* Mark Twain *were yanked from their routes and sent north to become Advance Zephyrs. Here is* Injun Joe, Huckleberry Finn, *and* Tom Sawyer *minus the* Becky Thatcher *baggage car leaving Denver for Chicago on June 12, 1936, giving Denverites a taste of modern streamlined travel. (Denver Public Library, Otto Perry Collection)*

The Mark Twain *9903 waits in the Denver train station as passengers board and the mail and baggage are loaded for the long haul to Chicago. This Advance Zephyr was a scheme to begin the Denver to Chicago route before the two Denver Zephyr trains were assembled at Budd. Sharing the route with the four-car* Pioneer, *this three-car* Injun Joe *train was a temporary measure to begin cranking up revenue. (Denver Public Library, Otto Perry Collection)*

roller bearings were added to the journal designs to further smooth out the ride. Each truck was individually balanced according to its expected load, varying from 94,543 lbs for the 36-inch wheel power truck to the last 30-inch truck on the *Tom Sawyer* parlor car that supported 32,550 lbs.

Every Zephyr up to the *Mark Twain* was set up this way – as a unified articulated design that coordinated all the train's elements into a unique specimen of rail transportation. As demand for more Zephyrs continued to swell, flaws in this concept that were minor annoyances with the *Pioneer Zephyr* became major frustrations.

The three-car *Pioneer* no longer supported its passenger demand, so a 40-seat

Minus its baggage car, the Mark Twain Zephyr rolls at 10 mph, obeying the yard limit as it passes a steam-servicing facility with coaling tower in St. Louis on August 16, 1940. Alongside the Zephyr is an old Atlantic steamer, former high-stepping speed queen of the main-line varnish runs. Now it waits as the gray ash is hosed off its smoke box. (Denver Public Library, Otto Perry Collection)

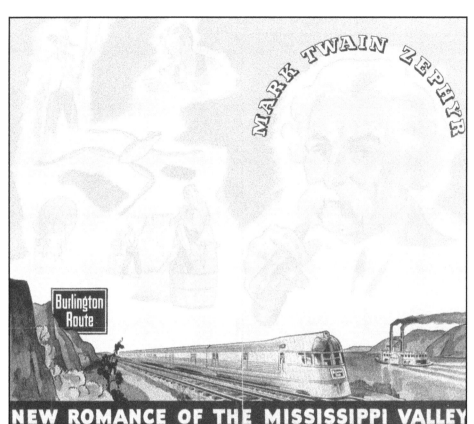

NEW ROMANCE OF THE MISSISSIPPI VALLEY

The Mark Twain Zephyr was the object of much schmaltz in the CB&Q PR department. This brochure, heralding the "New Romance of the Mississippi Valley," shows the shovel-nose streamliner howling downriver ahead of a string of stainless-steel coaches stretching into the horizon while an old riverboat beats upriver, slapping the water with a paddle wheel. With that many coaches hanging off Injun Joe *and its single Winton diesel engine, the riverboat would win any race between the two. (Burlington Route Historical Society)*

type articulated train-set concept, other Class One railroads with the same short-haul revenue problems as the Burlington failed to buy into the idea. The inflexibility of articulation was one sore point. For example, the train required a "wye" at each of its route-ends to turn back in the other direction. A wye is a track arrangement that works like an auto's three-point turn to reverse direction and looks like the letter "Y" when viewed from above. Despite proven success on the main line and in the Burlington's coffers, the diesel-electric was still looked upon as suitable for yard-goat switchers or jumped-up trolley cars running commuter routes. The exception to this blind eye was the Boston & Maine.

Combining a decent kitchen with a famous celebrity name produced this elegantly embossed menu handed out at the inaugural run of the Mark Twain Zephyr. By shuffling space priorities, Burlington and Budd made room for the kitchen in three cars, outdoing the Pioneer's *simple buffet grill. Stuffing the steam generator into the* Huckleberry Finn *kitchen-dinette-smoking car coach allowed the* Twain *to lose the* Becky Thatcher *baggage car for a faster road trip with no loss of amenities. (Dave Lotz Collection)*

chair car was added in June 1935. Following that upgrade was a 40-seat dinette buffet car in June 1938, and a 60-seat chair car was shoehorned into the 9902 *Twin Zephyr* in 1939. The CB&Q even found it necessary to move these additional cars around to other Zephyr routes where service did not require the high-speed runs. Increased capacity and 100 mph sprints were incompatible with the original 600-hp Winton 201A diesel engines.

When the *Mark Twain Zephyr* was ready for its service runs, the CB&Q's PR department wanted one last shot at headlines. To prep the train, it was put in service on the Twin Cities run from Minneapolis to Chicago. On October 13, 1935, the train covered the 882 miles in 12 hours. As with the *Pioneer* and *Twins*, the *Mark Twain* finally took off

on a high-speed run for the press. In order to maximize the speed, the four-car train lost the *Becky Thatcher* baggage car at the West Burlington shops to become a three-car train. When the dust settled and everyone had found their hat, the stopwatches and mile markers had registered a top speed of 122 mph for a distance of three consecutive miles.

With *Becky Thatcher* reattached between *Injun Joe* and *Huckleberry Finn*, the *Mark Twain Zephyr* went into service on October 28, 1935, between Burlington, Iowa, and St. Louis, Missouri, as trains No. 43 (northbound) and 44 (southbound). At Burlington, the *Mark Twain* connected with the *Aristocrat*, an east/west bound steam-hauled passenger train.

Despite all the tub-thumping and ballyhoo Budd initiated for the Zephyr-

CHAPTER SIX

THE *FLYING YANKEE* 6000

This heavily colored and airbrushed postcard rendition of the 6000 Flying Yankee taking on passengers at Old Orchard Beach, Maine, gives some indication of its star status among Maine attractions during its lifetime. (Courtesy, Flying Yankee Restoration Group)

N amed the *Flying Yankee*, the CB&Q's Budd three-car articulated diesel-electric train, No. 6000, was virtually identical to the *Pioneer Zephyr* and the original *Twin Zephyrs*. The layout differed in that it maximized passenger space by including seats behind the reduced-size baggage compartment in the power car. Like the other Zephyrs, the *Yankee* was a child of the Depression, and like that child it was handed around from relative to relative once a good impression was made. It retained the *Flying Yankee* name along its route from Boston's North Station to Bangor.

Exploiting all the value-added extras of the growing Zephyr fleet and taking the ever-popular tour around the system, the *Yankee's* reward was an instant jump in passenger ticket sales. From April 1, 1935, the three-car shovelnose became a fixture on Maine and, later, New Hampshire short-run trackage.

As it was shuttled from route to route, the name on the nose panel changed. From Boston to Bangor, it was the *Flying Yankee*; from Boston to Littleton, New Hampshire, via Crawford Notch, the train became the *Mountaineer*. Traveling the schedule from Boston to White River Junction via Keene, it became the *Cheshire*. Assuming the identity of *Minuteman*, the phantom streamliner traveled between Boston and Troy, New York. Finally, showing its age before retirement, the train set was known as the *Businessman*. Wherever it went, increases in passenger revenue followed. And regardless of the name on the nose of the power car, the plaques on the rear of the parlor car always read *Flying Yankee*.

Because of its eventual resurrection, the *Flying Yankee* is relevant

Diners in the 9900 Zephyr or Flying Yankee *coach sections made use of diagonally cantilevered trays that slid into these slots at the base of each seat. The entire tray and its supports were removed after the meal. (Gerry Souter Photo)*

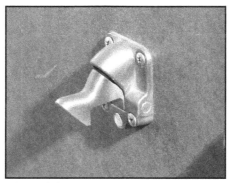

Aboard the Flying Yankee *and* Zephyrs *were many small details that were nonetheless carefully sculpted as design pieces. Typical is this door-holder latch in the entry-exit vestibule between cars. It is made of separate brass castings polished to a high shine and very Art Deco in execution. (Gerry Souter Photo)*

beyond its significance as the only Budd diesel shovelnose that didn't belong to the Burlington. The original *Pioneer Zephyr* train set is a static display at the Chicago Museum of Science and Industry. The last power car of the fleet, the *Silver Charger*, rests outside on a stub-track display in the Museum of Transportation outside St.

Small touches with even the most plebian accessories kept heads turning during a ride on the Budd Flying Yankee *or* Zephyr*. Each train was unique concerning interior appointments, but thought was given to simple functional items such as this radiating-vein lamp enclosure above the exit-entry vestibule. A simple single-chamber enclosure would have done the job, but the designer went the next step to maximize illumination from the single bulb. (Gerry Souter Photo)*

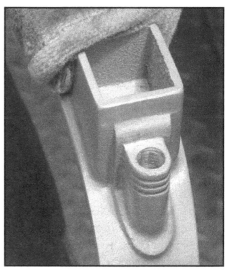

Since each parlor-car chair was individual, trays for meals slid into this round receptacle. The square receptacle, also cast into the chair arm, was for a slide-out ashtray, replacing the weighted floor stands. (Gerry Souter Photo)

The Boston & Maine Flying Yankee was an important project for Budd. He hoped other railroads would buy into the streamline-diesel concept. This ad that appeared in Time Magazine on October 5, 1936, describes the first year of Flying Yankee operation, citing 225,439 miles at 740 miles a day transporting 95,524 passengers. The Yankee mirrored the success of the Zephyrs, which it followed in 1935. (Courtesy, Flying Yankee *Restoration Group*)

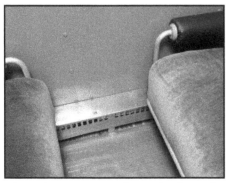

Floor heaters ran down both walls, radiating heat upward and guaranteeing passengers at least one very warm foot to face Maine winters for Yankee passengers and the Midwest chills for Zephyr riders. An individual car thermostat in the charge of the conductor controlled the heaters. (Gerry Souter Photo)

The Flying Yankee *parlor car waits for work to be finished on the power car now taking up shop space. Stripped to its metal, the car reveals the manufacturing processes that went into all Budd shovelnose streamliners of this period. It is a virtual textbook of modern metallurgy at work during that period. (Gerry Souter Photo)*

The fine burling in this hardwood windowsill shows the lengths Budd went to create a first-class environment for passengers that would also endure hard use and keep its good looks. This window is in the coach of the Flying Yankee, being restored to running order in New Hampshire. (Gerry Souter Photo)

Louis. "We fire her up once and a while," said one of the museum's volunteers, "just to keep those engines in operating order. Wouldn't take much to put her back on the main line again."

The *Flying Yankee*, however, has aspirations to outlive the entire shovel-nose fleet as the only operating, schedule-keeping, passenger-carrying example of these transportation pioneers.

The *Yankee* now rests in three pieces in a restoration shop in Claremont, New Hampshire. The power car and parlor car have been stripped to their stainless-steel

Caught rolling through the urban landscape is the Boston & Maine – Maine Central No. 6000 Flying Yankee's kinship to the CB&Q Zephyrs is evident in this postcard. The Yankee was a popular, high-visibility showpiece in the East as its cousins were in the Corn Belt and out West. (Courtesy, Flying Yankee Restoration Group)

Side steps were built into the lower-body full-fluted skirting that ran down all three cars. Their height was set to an average for most station platforms. (Gerry Souter Photo)

shells, but the passenger coach has been lovingly restored to its former glory. All the cars rest on temporary trucks originally built for 44-tonner diesel switchers until their new custom ORYX-designed wheel sets arrive. The state of New Hampshire owns the train and is cooperating with the *Flying Yankee* Restoration Group

(info@flyingyankee.com) to put the *Yankee* back on its wheels as a tourist attraction and educational asset. Known in the East as the B&M No. 6000, the shovelnose streamliner retired as the *Minuteman* in May 1957 with 2.75 million miles on its clock. With a little fix-up from its fans, the *Flying Yankee* seems to have many more miles left to go.

Demand Builds the Fleet

Back in the Burlington front office, all was joy and the jingle of new revenue. Four Zephyr shovelnoses were charging back and forth along their scheduled runs packed with pleased passengers. They were achieving 94 percent on-time performance compared with 60 percent for the coal-burners hauling heavyweight passenger varnish on other short-trip hauls. Streamlining and diesel-electric power combined with luxurious accommodations had proved a success with the

public. The only improvement could be more of the same. The CB&Q had two options and exercised both at the same time.

Since the world record-breaking run from Denver to Chicago in 1934, that route was begging for Zephyr service. But longer trains were needed to handle the estimated passenger load. That meant overcoming the current Zephyr's two major shortcomings – insufficient motive power and the growing curse of articulation. The same problems bedeviled the *Twin Zephyrs* racing back and forth between the Twin Cities and Chicago.

Determined to keep the Zephyrs' efficient and profitable record intact, Ralph Budd committed to purchase new shovelnose trains.

Not quite ready to totally abandon the articulated train set concept, the CB&Q decided to push it to an extreme by adding sets to the Twin Cities trains and increasing the power car's horsepower to haul them.

Here is a view down the aisle of the restored Flying Yankee coach. Indirect lighting illuminates the ceiling. Note the hat racks and wide windows. Each pair of seats rests in a cast tubular frame without robe racks on the seat backs. The armrests are circular and wrapped with what was leather then and is vinyl now. (Gerry Souter Photo)

A fully-restored parlor car chair with its plush upholstery, cast frame, and square ashtray holder behind the round tray table receptacle is one of the group that lines the Flying Yankee parlor-observation car wall. Budd tinkered with these chairs throughout the life of the shovelnose fleet, making each iteration a bit more luxurious. (Gerry Souter Photo)

The restored Flying Yankee, now owned by the State of New Hampshire, will act as a goodwill state booster loaded with audio-visual information for tourist riders. This cable transition box between cars was not original equipment, but is part of the Yankee's new role and the A/V hardware needed to fulfill it. (Gerry Souter Photo)

The old and the new are combined here to show the articulation mechanism cast for the end of each connected car and a cable-connection box for modern inter-car and audio-visual communication. Once the Flying Yankee is restored to operational status, it will become a traveling tourist attraction for the state of New Hampshire, complete with a video and audio-visual story. (Courtesy, Flying Yankee Restoration Group, Gerry Souter Photo)

Today's Flying Yankee *parlor car* waits its turn for a makeover. Meanwhile, all original truck-side frames and wheel sets are out getting their own facelifts. To fill in, the Flying Yankee Restoration Group has the cars propped up on trucks scavenged from old 44-tonner diesel switcher locomotives painted silver to give some semblance of the originals. (Gerry Souter Photo)

At the rear of the Flying Yankee's parlor car reside the running lights that, while not faired into the contour of the roofline, at least present a minimal bulge to the slipstream. (Gerry Souter Photo)

As the Flying Yankee sat about, quietly rotting before being slated for restoration to full operation, corrosion did manage to weaken even the stainless-steel support system buried behind aging and often sodden Masonite wall panels. Rather than rebuild in stainless, the restorers hand-fashioned wood supports over the steel arching forms to achieve the proper thickness. (Gerry Souter Photo)

Halted at the station at Nashua, New Hampshire, in 1935, the Flying Yankee draws its usual crowd. Note the ventilator just beyond the roof slope. It is just above the Yankee's buffet grill and just past the minimal baggage space. Compare with the Mark Twain Zephyr's Becky Thatcher car – one big baggage space. (Courtesy, Flying Yankee Restoration Group)

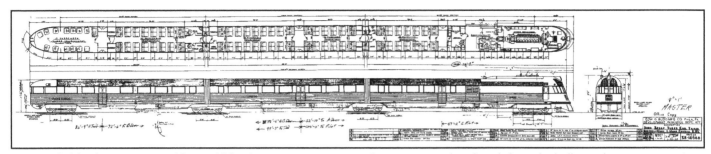

A remarkable diagram created by Budd for the Boston & Maine and Maine Central Railroads based wholly on the Pioneer Zephyr, showing as it does every filler cap and steam line terminus – some things that might not appear on a preliminary proposal drawing for a "High Speed Train." Many of the corrections are there, too, such as the two-man cab, learned from the Pioneer Zephyr. In the Flying Yankee, the two railroad shoppers were getting a tried-and-true winner. (Courtesy, Flying Yankee Restoration Group)

Just as the Pioneer and Twin Zephyrs changed names depending on where they were needed, the Flying Yankee swept all over the Northeast under different guises. Here, it's the Mountaineer near North Conway, New Hampshire, in July 1938. Later in its career, it became the Businessman. Note that the cook has left his buffet grill to catch a smoke out the baggage room door. (Courtesy, Flying Yankee Restoration Group)

Though not comparable to the CB&Q public relations machine, the combined efforts of the Boston & Maine and Maine Central Railroads managed to circulate some engaging brochures and fliers to stir up interest. This booklet came out in 1935, extolling the virtues of their diesel streamliner. (Courtesy, Flying Yankee Restoration Group)

The Flying Yankee *heads out on its run between Boston and Bangor, Maine, on July 16, 1935. The service was a rousing success though, curiously, the* Yankee *had the smallest-capacity baggage room of all the shovelnoses. Baggage only occupied a small area just behind the engine compartment just in front of the buffet, and considerable passenger space. (Courtesy,* Flying Yankee *Restoration Group)*

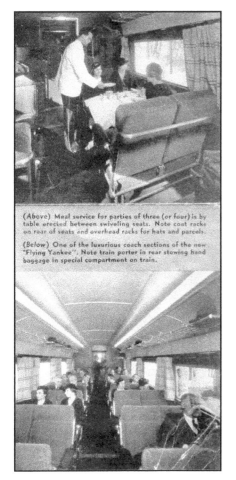

(Above) Meal service for parties of three (or four) is by table erected between swiveling seats. Note coat racks on rear of seats and overhead racks for hats and parcels.

(Below) One of the luxurious coach sections of the new "Flying Yankee". Note train porter in rear stowing hand baggage in special compartment on train.

With snow on the ground, passengers aboard the Flying Yankee *enjoy a meal from the buffet as they rush along their 740-mile journey between Boston and Bangor, Maine. Fold-up tables were available for parties of four, otherwise tray tables slid into seat-mounted castings. Note the coat racks on the window wall, the linen, and silver. Below, in this brochure, passengers watch the scenery roll past while a porter stows some belongings. Note the horizontal-striped draperies. (Courtesy,* Flying Yankee *Restoration Group)*

This 1935 brochure has the nice messy quality of candid photography and these people in the parlor car are definitely not models. The car has a lived-in look showing how 12 people could fit in there for a 700-mile trip and entertain themselves without television. Below, we glimpse at how the cantilevered seat trays fit into the castings built into the seat as a steward stands poised. Behind him is the buffet from which all good things flow. (Courtesy, Flying Yankee *Restoration Group)*

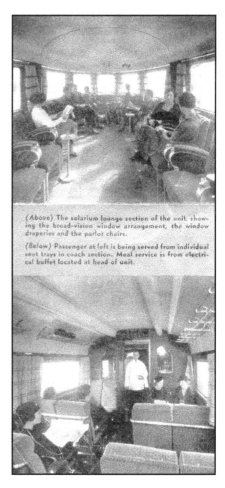

(Above) The solarium lounge section of the unit, showing the broad-vision window arrangement, the window draperies and the parlor chairs.

(Below) Passenger at left is being served from individual seat trays in coach section. Meal service is from electrical buffet located at head of unit.

CHAPTER SEVEN

THE *DENVER ZEPHYRS*
9906–9907

With the blinds drawn and the world outside hammering past at 90 mph, there's nary a ripple in a water glass in the Denver Zephyr's dining room. Note all those tools, butter dishes, and relish trays – each setting for dinner was first-class. If the diners seem overdressed, they're not. People dressed up to ride the train, especially the Zephyr. Note the accessorized and mirrored buffet alcove behind the waiter. Every meal featured custom-designed china and flatware, kept sparkling in the full kitchen built into the Denver Zephyr's food-preparation area. (BNSF Photo)

The 1,034-mile *Denver Zephyr* run to Chicago posed the greatest risk because no diesel-electric engine had ever powered a high-capacity train over that much track. Would the CB&Q's maintenance program be up to the task? A train of 10 cars plus the power car was visualized, plus triple the passenger payload of the four-car units. If articulation was completely eliminated, all those extra car wheels – eight under each car – would add to the track friction and the required hauling effort, cutting fuel economy and obviously requiring considerably more power than the current 600-hp Winton 201A engine. The design solution had to pack more than a few compromises.

The first problem to solve for the proposed *Denver Zephyr* with its 10-car, 1,000-mile run was adequate power to sustain expected high speeds plus bursts up in the century digits. When the engineers' slide rules finished clacking back and forth, it was determined that 3,000 hp

would deliver Zephyr-like speed characteristics.

Diesel engine design had moved along creating a number of efficient possibilities. The Electro-Motive Corporation that had absorbed Winton now had a roster of possible engine combinations. In August 1935, V-12 versions of the original straight-eight Winton 201A put out 900 hp. Two of them were combined for a trio of box-cab passenger locomotives for GE and two locomotives for St. Louis Car, transferring 1,800 hp to the track. A double-headed front end on the *Denver Zephyr* with this configuration provided 3,600 hp. That was too many horses and too many engines.

Ultimately, Budd and Electro-Motive decided on double-heading the Zephyr with an A unit with the operators' cab powered by a pair of 900-hp V-12 diesel engines putting out 1,800 hp attached to a B unit running a brand-new 1,200-hp V-16. The B unit had no cab and was operated from the A unit, having only minimum yard-hostler controls to move it about for maintenance.

To whet the appetites of Denver-to-Chicago potential passengers, the CB&Q yanked the Mark Twain and the Pioneer Zephyr (four-car version) off their runs to stand in for the two new Zephyrs under construction. Regardless of the lack of sleeping accommodations, the rudimentary food service, and the crowding, the runs on the short, fast streamliners were solidly booked. By the time the Denver Zephyrs, 9906–9907, showed up, there were plenty of fans to greet them. (Burlington Route Historical Society)

The Zephyrs were popular subjects for postcards. The CB&Q encouraged the image in any media from toy models to postcards to appearing in popular movies. The Zephyrs' distinctive look made them a poster child for "the future of transportation" along with the Boeing DC-3 airliner and Lincoln Zephyr automobile. (Dave Lotz Collection)

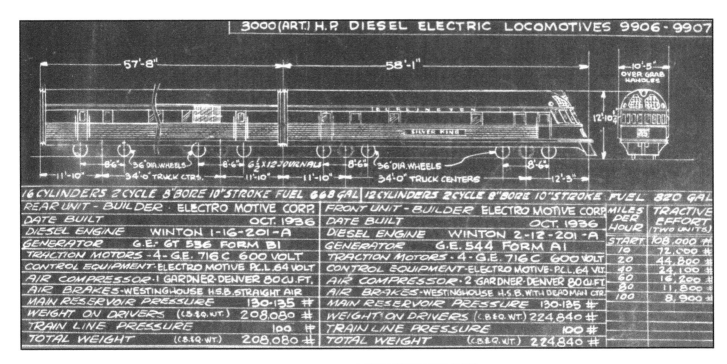

3000(ART.) H.P. DIESEL ELECTRIC LOCOMOTIVES 9906-9907		

16 CYLINDERS 2 CYCLE 8"BORE 10"STROKE FUEL 668 GAL	12 CYLINDERS 2 CYCLE 8"BORE 10"STROKE FUEL 820 GAL		
REAR UNIT - BUILDER · ELECTRO MOTIVE CORP.	FRONT UNIT - BUILDER · ELECTRO MOTIVE CORP	MILES PER HOUR	TRACTIVE EFFORT (TWO UNITS)
DATE BUILT OCT. 1936	DATE BUILT OCT. 1936	START	108,000 #
DIESEL ENGINE WINTON 1-16-201-A	DIESEL ENGINE WINTON 2-12-201-A	10	72,000 #
GENERATOR G.E. GT 536 FORM B1	GENERATOR G.E. 544 FORM A1	20	44,800 #
TRACTION MOTORS - 4 · G.E. 716 C 600 VOLT	TRACTION MOTORS - 4 · G.E. 716 C 600 VOLT	40	24,100 #
CONTROL EQUIPMENT-ELECTRO MOTIVE P.C.L.64 VOLT	CONTROL EQUIPMENT-ELECTRO MOTIVE P.C.L.64 VLT	60	16,200 #
AIR COMPRESSOR·1 GARDNER-DENVER 80 CU.FT.	AIR COMPRESSOR · 2 GARDNER-DENVER 80 CU.FT	80	11,800 #
AIR BRAKES-WESTINGHOUSE H.S.B. STRAIGHT AIR	AIR BRAKES-WESTINGHOUSE H.S.B. WITH DEAD MAN CTR.	100	8,900 #
MAIN RESERVOIR PRESSURE 130-135 #	MAIN RESERVOIR PRESSURE 130-135 #		
WEIGHT ON DRIVERS (C.B.&Q.WT.) 208,080 #	WEIGHT ON DRIVERS (C.B.&Q.WT.) 224,840 #		
TRAIN LINE PRESSURE 100 #	TRAIN LINE PRESSURE 100 #		
TOTAL WEIGHT (C.B.&Q.WT.) 208,080 #	TOTAL WEIGHT (C.B.&Q.WT.) 224,840 #		

Gracing this dual-function postcard and schedule, the Denver Zephyr is shown joining the Chicago metropolis with the Colorado Rockies. With stops at Omaha and Lincoln, the sleeper- and dining room-outfitted streamliner fulfilled the Zephyr concept begun in 1934. (Burlington Route Historical Society)

The powerhouses of the Zephyr fleet, the Denver Zephyrs, 9906 and 9907, were double-headed diesels using two cars as one power unit, both operated from the cab. This blueprint varies from the others in that the second car is included and the stats doubled. The head-end control car carried a pair of V-12, 900-hp EMC/Winton engines, while the second car added a new V-16 diesel producing 1,200 hp. Note that two standard 36-inch-diameter four-wheel trucks were employed, but with the wheelbases lengthened by six inches. This train also inaugurated the "silver" series for the Burlington with the Silver King and Silver Knight locomotives leading long lines of "silver" coaches. (Burlington Route Historical Society)

As mentioned earlier, at this point the locomotive engineers' and firemen's unions threw up their hands and dusted off their negotiating hats. If it had an engine, it needed a full crew. This was one of the earliest A-B unit labor tests. Cosmetically no train identification number was painted on the B units, making them "part" of the A units.

The shovelnose A-B unit laid down exactly 3,000 hp. With that much juice on the front end, articulation only needed minimizing, not elimination, to maintain speeds and introduce some train make-up flexibility. The two *Denver Zephyrs*, 9906 and 9907, were each made up of six complete sections comprised of either single cars or dual artic-

ulated units. Ohio Brass Tight-lock couplers were used:

- Between the two locomotive units
- Between the second loco unit and the first car
- Between the first and second cars
- Between the fifth and sixth articulated body units

The Silver Queen, *9906B, followed the* Denver Zephyr Silver King *everywhere in revenue service, connected by a pair of Ohio Brass Tight-lock couplers. However, for maintenance purposes, the 1,200-hp-powered* Queen *was often separated from the* King. *A minimum set of controls was provided for the yard "hostler," as the maintenance crewman was called, as well as a window to work the car into the shop or work track. Also note a separate set of dual horns. (Jim Singer Collection)*

Normally, the rear end of a diesel locomotive would be of little interest except this is a Burlington Zephyr split into two power units. This front end, the Silver King, *carried a pair of 900-hp Winton engines, one of which can be seen through the open door and was connected to the* Silver Queen, *which hauled a V-12 1,600-hp engine needed to drag the longest Zephyr consist. (Jim Singer Collection)*

These couplers do not permit the coaches to separate and climb over each other, minimizing casualties in case of an accident. They also avoided problems of loose couplers between cars. An engineer could make a full brake application without worrying about slack-action between couplers causing a chain reaction down the line.

Articulated or semi-permanent drawbar connections were made:

• Between the second and third units
• Between the seventh and eighth units
• Between the ninth and tenth units

This step away from full articulation allowed either dual-car units or single cars to be added or subtracted from a train. By the end of the 1930s virtually every railroad that had tried articulation abandoned the practice. Later, in the modern era, super high-speed trains returned to articulation using wheel pairs between cars linking together train sets in "Talgo" configurations. Old railroad men shook their heads as the computerized designers trotted out their math to show the efficiency of the concept.

Meanwhile, back with the *Denver Zephyrs,* the CB&Q was impatient to begin the service to Chicago. The front office yanked the 9900 *Pioneer* and 9903 *Mark Twain Zephyrs* from their local runs to become the *Advance Zephyrs* between Denver and Chicago. The little four-car trains were swamped with ticket sales as the shotwelders in the Budd and Electro-Motive shops popped away, building the new stainless-steel cars and motive power for the long-range shovelnoses.

The orders were placed in December 1935 and the work divided between Budd, who framed up the cars at their Philadelphia plant as they had done with the previous Zephyrs, and a new Electro-Motive McCook plant near LaGrange, Illinois, where the motive power and accessories were installed and sides, ends, and roofs were attached. This interchange between builders signaled the growing efficiency of parts standardization that helped prove the diesel-electric ascendancy over steam power.

Scruffy-looking without its final cleanup, the Silver King *rests on the turnaround wye outside Electro-Motive's new LaGrange plant at McCook, Illinois, on October 4, 1936. Note the front coupler has been installed for maneuvering the locomotive during fit-out. Though the front-coupler panel was screwed in place during service, each Zephyr carried at least one knuckle coupler on board for emergency tows or yard work. Most of the body framing had been accomplished at the Budd plant in Philadelphia, but EMC made the two* Denver Zephyrs *on their own in the final stages of construction. (Jim Singer Collection)*

On October 16, 1936, the Zephyrs 9906A and B rolled out of the LaGrange shops followed a few days later by 9907A and B. They were lettered *Denver Zephyrs* in red on each side of the power car's nose. Continuing with the *Mark Twain's* "naming" of the cars, the 9906A and B were christened the *Silver King* and *Silver Queen* while 9907A and B bore the monikers *Silver Knight* and *Silver Princess*. In the quaintly innocent 1930s, the more powerful, controlling, front-end lead power unit with the headlight had a male name, while the sub-missive, controlled, trailing, less powerful booster unit was a lady.

On October 24, 1936, another lady figured in the launching of the *Denver Zephyr*. Jane Cody Garlow, granddaughter of Buffalo Bill Cody, saddled up a paint horse and in full cowboy regalia let fly with a bottle of champagne tethered by a long ribbon to the grillwork of the gleaming shovelnose. Two weeks later, on November 8, that train rolled out of Denver and blazed its way to Chicago in 15 hours and 20 minutes. In Chicago, Ms. Garlow got to bash the Zephyr once again with a jug of bubbly, and then official service began between the two cities.

The 10-car "Silver" train that stretched out behind those power units was the ultimate expression of Ralph Budd and Edward Budd's original concept for the streamliner of the future. From their signature shovelnose to their rounded tail ends, no luxurious, state-of-the-art feature had been spared.

There was room on board for 309 passengers, some sat in 102 coach seats while others snoozed in the 93 upper and lower berths. This first-time-ever use of sleeper units under the Zephyr name offered two 12-section sleeper cars and one car fitted out with compartments and bedrooms.

A "section sleeper" is a car that provides facing bench sofas that convert into lower berths, and a swing-down upper berth from above the windows. Each section was then curtained off from the aisle. These low-cost overnight accommodations originated by Pullman in the 19th century were eventually replaced by "roomettes" and other inexpensive – but more private – configurations in passenger trains following the war.

Dining and lounge facilities on the Zephyr provided seats for 104 passengers, plus 10 single seats in the parlor section. Sixteen chairs and three loveseats occupied the observation car and there were even 31 seats scattered through the men's and women's dressing rooms and restrooms.

A full side view of the Denver Zephyr Silver King *as it awaits final polish, and engine fit-out clearly shows the refined roofline created by Budd designers as a culmination of the streamlined look. Also, the roof is smooth, not fluted, matching the window piers and leaving the fluting for lower side-panel decoration. Note the long-wheelbase four-wheel power trucks, both with 36-inch-diameter wheels with axles tied to a pair of Winton 900-hp engines. (Jim Singer Collection)*

From the 20th Street viaduct at the Denver passenger station, Otto Perry caught the 9907 Silver Knight *and* Silver Princess *ready to pull out with 10 cars full of passengers heading east to Chicago on August 27, 1938. Note the front windows and side door are open for ventilation during slow-speed yard travel. This angle also shows both sets of stacks in the* Knight *and the single set in the roof of the* Princess *for her V-16 engine. Compare the autos in the lot with the Zephyr to appreciate the streamliner's radical design for its time. (Denver Public Library, Otto Perry photograph)*

A tour from the shovelnose through the 10 cars reveals designers at work mastering an intense learning curve from the original *Pioneer Zephyr* 9900. The most striking changes, aside from the new cars and services provided, were the variety of color and decoration schemes. Earlier day-tripper Zephyrs kept to a palette of blues, creams, pearls, pale greens, and buffs, highlighted with touches of gold and the shine of aluminum banding. The *Denver Zephyr* rushed through a variety of landscapes and took its decoration cues from them all – from rich earth, wood, and rock colors to the hues of the big skies and river waters touched by wild flowers and the historic riches of the gold and silver strikes. This environment of harmonious colors and variety of tactile textures was encased in streamlined stainless-steel capsules that reflected the emerging modern era. As 19th-century

passenger accommodations layered on the wood paneling, overstuffed chairs with antimacassars, glass-beaded gaslight fixtures, ornate iron stoves, and plush Berber carpeting underfoot, they were products of their time, like grand old Victorian ladies, clanking down the rails at a sedate and dignified speed.

On October 23, 1936, the three diesel engines driving the *Denver Zephyr* 9906 A and B units with 3,000 hp lanced across the landscape heading a six-car train at an average speed of 83.33 mph with a burst of 116 mph while barely rippling the surface of a sloe gin fizz.

Up front in the A unit sat the driver and fireman fighting the hypnotic trance-like doze induced by the blurring ribbon of rails and ties passing just beneath their feet. Between them sat the GE GT-544 generator-end of one of the V-12 201A engines developing 900 hp.

That generator powered two GE 716C 600-volt traction motors. A second V-12 201A engine, also putting out 900 hp, faced in the other direction and filled the rest of the 58-foot unit. Each engine could be operated separately if needed. Auxiliary power flowing from the A unit provided 220-volt, three-phase, 60-cycle electricity to run lighting, air conditioning, and refrigeration. Assorted tanks carried 820 gallons of diesel, 150 gallons of lubricating oil, 410 gallons of cooling water, and 16 cubic feet of sand to spray beneath the wheels for traction on hills and to aid braking on slippery track.

Above this pair of howling engines and whining generators, the original stainless roof had been altered to a single, non-fluted sweeping line from the headlight to the observation car instead of the fluted raised cab line of the *Pioneer, Twins,* and *Mark Twain* units. Beneath

Buttoned up at speed, the Denver Zephyr Silver King 9906 and Silver Queen rush toward Chicago with all three engines churning. By the time of the Denver Zephyrs the vision of high-speed travel had other railroads buying the new lightweight cars and hiding their steam engines under aluminum shrouds. (Jim Singer Collection)

Posed for its official photograph, the Silver Knight 9907 and Silver Princess 9907A shimmer in the morning sun as the engineer, fireman, and a civilian passenger, possibly a roadmaster, regard the cameraman. As the Zephyr series grew so did the cab accommodations from a single engineer in 1934 to three-abreast seating in the 1938 Silver Charger 9908. (D. L. Hopwood photo, Jim Singer Collection)

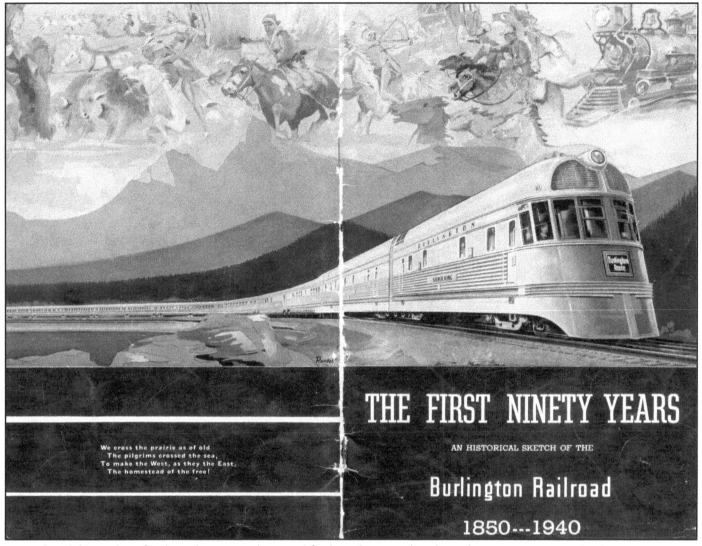

THE FIRST NINETY YEARS

AN HISTORICAL SKETCH OF THE

Burlington Railroad

1850---1940

We cross the prairie as of old
The pilgrims crossed the sea,
To make the West, as they the East,
The homestead of the free!

Artists loved the Zephyrs for their elegant simplicity and for how the trains lent themselves to exaggeration (or "artistic interpretation"). Here, one of the Denver Zephyrs graces the cover of a "historical sketch of the Burlington Railroad 1850 – 1940." The Zephyr stretches its 10-car train sinuously around a western landscape beneath a sky full of imagined pioneer action: "We cross the prairie as of old – the pilgrims crossed the sea, To make the West, as they the East, the homestead of the free!" There was no end of this Manifest Destiny hoopla as the Burlington dueled the Santa Fe for ownership of the West. (Burlington Route Historical Society)

Two elements tip off this photo as an early pre-service shot of the 9906 Silver King Denver Zephyr. The lettering, which appears white in the photo, is actually in red, which was later changed to standard black. The other tip-off is the location of the sand-loading hatch just ahead of the second side window. This hatch was for loading sand that was sprayed beneath the wheels for additional traction when necessary. It was later relocated to the top of the pier panel between the first window and the door. (Burlington Route Historical Society)

the roof, as with the *Pioneer*, the cooling radiator tubes clung to the ceiling.

The 224,840-lb A unit rode on a four-wheel power truck with 36-inch wheels nestled between Timken roller bearings and ended it riding a second set of trucks and Tight-lock couplers securing it to the following B unit. This connection made it the first non-articulated A unit built by Electro-Motive that didn't have cabs at both ends.

Following obediently, the B unit motored along with a V-16 201A engine adding 1,200 hp to the power train and driving a GE GT-536 generator that fed four GE-716C traction motors. Entering the unit amid the cacophony of thundering diesels you passed between a pair of Clarkson CA4160 steam boilers that could generate 1,600 lbs of steam per hour to keep out the Rocky Mountain cold and prairie chills before bucking Chicago winters.

Almost 1,000 gallons of diesel could be accommodated in the B unit along with 95 gallons of lube oil and another 16 cubic feet of sand. Known as "box cars" or "tractors" by old CB&Q

hands, the B units weighed 208,080 lbs and were 4 inches shorter than the 58-foot A units.

The first actual train car behind the locomotive pair opened into four diesel-powered generators that supplied power for lighting, battery charging, air conditioning, ventilation, radios, refrigeration, and the telephone circuit. Each Cummins 85-hp, six-cylinder diesel engine powered a GE 50 kW, three-phase, 60-cycle, 220-volt generator. The juice traveled down an electric line to the Frigidaire air conditioners consisting of compressors and condensers under the floor of each car as well as the food refrigerators and icemakers in each preparation area.

Lighting was, for the most part, indirect, reflecting off false ceilings and from inside stainless fixtures. Ductwork carried cool air through the ceiling spaces and each car had its own thermostats for both cooling and heating. To keep sleepers cool in the section cars, additional openings were available for both upper and lower berths, each controllable by shifting shutters to direct the air. The

lighting system in the section sleepers was unique because of the physical separation of each sleeper bay by a partial wall partition. Center aisle ceiling lights in both direct and indirect fixtures marched the length of the car while individual reading lights were mounted on the walls of each section for reading illumination once the beds were made and curtains drawn. A five-kilovolt amp, single-phase transformer was located in each car. It managed the load of the three-phase current running in the train line so 32-volt secondary lighting could operate alongside 110-volt taps for electric shavers in the men's bathroom, hair dryers, drink mixers, and any other appliances that could plug into a standard wall socket.

At the other end of the electrical spectrum, if any emergency blew out the 220-volt AC power spine, battery power – always kept charged – took over until the AC was restored. With full power up and running, the DC battery supply switched off and recharged until needed again. Curiously, descriptions of this complex electrical system clash depending on whose explanation you read. Holland Wagner, writing in the *Burlington Bulletin* No. 13, Fourth Quarter in 1984, notes a discrepancy in the specs:

"Interestingly, original EMC specifications for all six of the 1936 units state that the A units had GE model 535 main generators and that the B units used GE 721 traction motors. All Burlington data, however, shows a 544 main generator in the As and 716C traction motors in both A and B units. And H. H. Urbach, head of the railroad's Mechanical Department, stated in a June 1939 presentation to the annual meeting of the Mechanical Division of the Association of American Railroads that the same type traction motors, pistons, connecting rods, injectors, cylinder liners, and cylinder heads are used in all sizes of (Zephyr) locomotives from the 600 hp to the 3,000 hp."

Resting quietly in the Denver railroad station, the 9906A and B have just broken the 9900 Pioneer Zephyr's 1934 record by racing from Chicago to Denver in 12 hours, 12 minutes, and 27 seconds at an average speed of 83 mph. On October 23, 1936, one week after their roll-out from the LaGrange plant, the King and Queen dropped off two sleeper cars to make the run and hauled eight coaches behind 3,000 hp. (Denver Public Library, Otto Perry Photo)

Early morning shadows stretch across the Electro-Motive workforce that assembled the Silver King and Queen 9906 Denver Zephyr completed on October 16, 1936. Only a week would pass before the locomotive would be joined to its train for a record-breaking run "uphill" from Chicago to Denver to re-create, in reverse, the run of the Pioneer Zephyr in 1934. Noting all the suits, this seems more of a "front office" bunch rather than the shotwelders and machinists who actually put the pieces together. (Jim Singer Collection)

Like any other part of the transportation industry from trains to autos to airplanes, each group has evolved through constant tinkering. As components wear out, new ones are fitted, retrofitted if the shop is lucky, or made to fit with torch and chisel if not. The big leaps in technology have happened less than the constant creeping changes that keep up with inventive minds and new challenges.

One of the most important electrical appliances aboard the *Denver Zephyr* was the Westinghouse electro-pneumatic train brake, controlled by a dead-man switch. This feature of the *Pioneer Zephyr* ostensibly removed the need for a second crewman. The brakes' functions had continued to develop. Besides braking, speed-control governors were attached to the second and 10th trucks. Because of the train's length and additional momentum to overcome, the

Only four days after breaking the 1934 Pioneer Zephyr speed run "in reverse" from Chicago to Denver, the Silver King 9906 and Silver Queen 9906A are parked at a service facility in Aurora, Illinois, just west of Chicago on October 27, 1936. Diesel fuel oil, two years earlier, had to be brought to the train in a tank truck. Eventually, diesel facilities were installed to bring oil to the under-frame tanks and sand to the side hatches. (Jim Singer Collection)

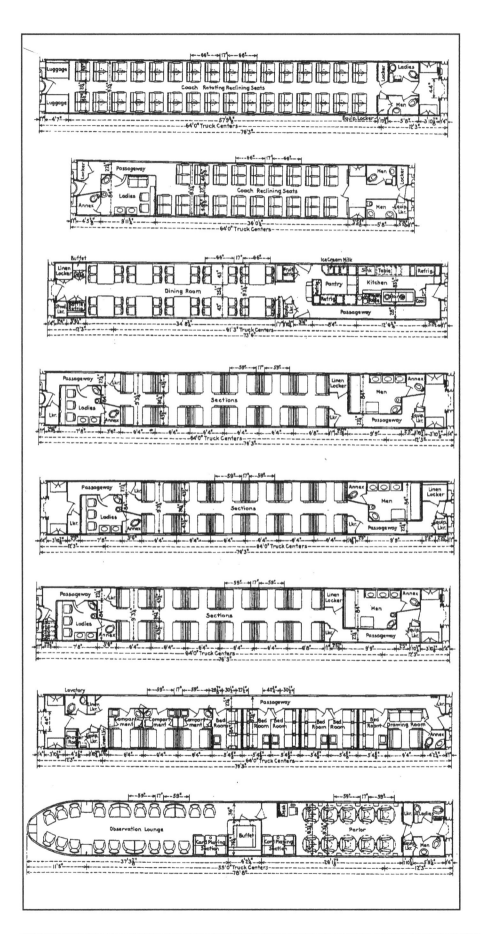

sander in the power car was supplemented by two additional sanders fitted to the third and seventh cars, adding grit to the rails for traction. These coaches had an outside filler door that could be filled by the hose from a steam engine facility-type sand tower or with a bucket from a trackside bin or dump truck. Until the Zephyr passenger service matured, diesel-servicing facilities had been rare and most commodities such as diesel fuel, sand, and lube oil were brought to trackside by trucks. As the efficiency and economy of the engines were proven, trackside service facilities began appearing in yards across the country.

Each car still rode on trucks mounting four 33-inch wheels cushioned with rubber pads and replacing the old swing-motion rollers and hangers with hydraulic cushioned shock absorbers to minimize side-to-side lateral sway. Heavy use of rubber padding also reduced sound transmission and vibration.

To ease maintenance and train servicing, the 10 revenue cars were

Named Pegasus, the 9904 power-car rolls out at the head of the Denver Zephyr train shown here leaving Denver, Colorado, on May 25, 1937. The power car runs off two 900-hp Winton diesel engines in order to move such a heavy consist at a spanking speed. It was identical to the Denver locomotives for which the Pegasus was often swapped out. The train is made up of a mix of independent coaches and articulated units. (Denver Public Library, Otto Perry Collection)

divided into six sections, each made up of articulated sets or combinations of independent coaches. This maintenance concept became necessary with the new long-distance trains and was carried over to the locomotives as well.

As the head of the Burlington's mechanical department, H.H. Urbach, said in his June 1939 speech to the American Association of Railroad's Mechanical Division,"...One 1,800-hp locomotive is entirely maintained at Chicago on a nine-hour, 45-minute layover. The two 3,000-hp locomotives are maintained at both Chicago and Denver. The layover is approximately eight hours. The maintenance work on these two locomotives is divided between the Chicago and Denver ter-

minals, and special facilities have been provided for the character of work performed at each of these terminals. The on-time performance of these four locomotives on the runs as stated above (Chicago-Minneapolis and Chicago-Denver) has been 96 percent. The availability of all the diesel road locomotives is 95 percent..."

Maintaining the Zephyrs allowed the CB&Q to innovate procedures unique to diesel motive power. In Chicago, for instance, a spare power truck was kept on hand that worked with either the 1,800-hp or 1,200-hp engines to provide quick-change backup against traction-motor failures. The changeovers were accomplished using special facilities fitted out with inspection pits, cranes, and an inventory of spare parts.

Quick turnaround also required refueling and refilling, which was accomplished at Denver, Minneapolis, and Chicago using special facilities to pump in the diesel fuel and dump the crankcase oil. On the *Denver Zephyr* run, an additional refueling stop had been added at Lincoln, Nebraska, where a crew change took place. This stop required only five minutes to pump in 1,700 gallons of diesel fuel.

Most delays in the scheduled runs that were caused by equipment failure had some form of backup. As the Burlington's Urbach went on tell AAR convention attendees in 1939, "...As each 1800-hp locomotive is equipped with two 900-hp diesel engines, where a failure occurs to a traction motor, con-

Passengers on the earliest *Pioneer Zephyr* could count on audio entertainment piped through the cars by means of an 11-tube Stromberg Carlson radio controlled by the conductor. Every passenger space had at least one pair of speakers built into the wall. As the number of cars on each train grew, until a dozen or more strung out behind the *Denver Zephyrs*, so did passenger requests for favorite radio programs, horse-race results, farm-product prices, and music.

Complaint letters began arriving at the CB&Q offices and operation memos shot out to division managers and train crews: "… many unfavorable comments have been made concerning soap operas, quiz programs, results of horse races, etcetera. Hereafter such programs are not to be carried."[12] To mollify sports fans, a separate radio was installed in the buffet car for World Series broadcasts, boxing matches, and special events.

To provide music in the cars, Webster and Armour wire recorders were installed that played back spools of prerecorded concerts of classical, swing, and dance music. Each spool held 7,200 feet of steel wire and played at 24 inches per second, reproducing an hour of recorded material. The quality would be considered "tinny" by today's standards, but the technology was very popular well into the 1950s when oxide-covered tape arrived. Webster wire reels were preferred over Armour because they, like the Zephyr train, were made of stainless steel so the music couldn't rust.

While the original wire recording technology traces back to 1878, it wasn't until 1930 when it was introduced as dictating machines and telephone recorders. They found extensive use during World War II for sending and recording clandestine messages between the Allies and resistance forces in Europe. From 1947 to 1952, wire recorders became popular in America and across Europe. The wire recorder was the first reliable audio recorder to find its way into the American home in significant numbers.

This 1940s consumer-model wire recorder was built by Sears Silvertone. It includes a 78-rpm record player, and the turntable is used as the take-up reel for the wire. Another interesting feature is how the record and playback head oscillates up and down to wind the wire evenly on the take-up reel. The Burlington employed wire recorders on the early Zephyr fleet for playback of prerecorded spools of music and special events. Ultimately, wire recording was replaced by oxide on tape developed by the Germans in World War II and brought back after the war to radio recording studios under the commercial name AMPEX. (Courtesy Phil Vourtsis Collection, Manalapan, New Jersey)

necting-rod bearing, piston, or cracked cylinder head, comparatively little time is lost with the other 900-hp engine handling the train, as compared to stopping the train and getting a steam loco-motive to handle. This same situation applies to the 3,000 hp, as these units are equipped with two 900-hp and one 1,200-hp diesel engines, and where a defective condition develops that makes it necessary to cut out one of the 900-hp units, comparatively little time is lost with the other two units in operation. If for some reason the 1,200-hp engine has to be cut out, it is then nec-

After almost four years of service scheduled train No. 10, the Denver Zephyr, 9907 Silver Knight *and* Silver Princess, *barrels across the flatlands east of Denver on March 16, 1940 just before sunset. Little has changed with the silver streamliner since its first run down these tracks on November 8, 1936. In 1951 the* King *and his* Queen *entered the Burlington's general passenger pool where, together with their* Twin Zephyr *lookalikes, they chugged along where needed until all had been dismantled by 1957. But in six years, their records had changed American passenger rail service forever. (Denver Public Library, Otto Perry Photograph)*

essary to use a steam locomotive to handle the train."

As with all the previous Zephyr routes, success bred further expansion. By 1938, however, articulation was a dead issue. The Q and a few other railroads had tried the system and, after experimentation, all of them abandoned the train set concept:

- Union Pacific M-10000 *City of Salina* (1934)
- New York, New Haven & Hartford *Comet* (1935)

- Union Pacific M-10001 *City of Portland* (1935)
- Illinois Central Railroad *Green Diamond* (1936)
- Chicago, Rock Island & Pacific *Peoria Rocket* (1937)

Budd also lost faith in the concept. If the power car was down, the train was down. Expanding or reducing a train's length meant a trip to the shop if an articulated train set was involved. The cars were noninterchangeable with any other cars in the

anticipated roster of non-articulated stainless-steel coaches. And, most important, if more cars were added to meet need, the engine could no longer take the strain. Budd had built its first non-articulated chair car, No. 3070, for the Santa Fe – in January 1936. Soon, non-articulated coaches were hooked up behind the CB&Q's *Aristocrat* between Denver and Chicago. Non-articulated cars were already mixed with two-car articulated sets on the *Denver Zephyrs*.

CHAPTER EIGHT

THE NEW TWIN CITIES ZEPHYRS 9904–9905

Decked out and adroitly airbrushed, one of the new seven-car Twin Cities Zephyrs poses for publicity handouts. The head-end locomotives (A-B) are the same as used with the Denver Zephyrs built months earlier with identical twin 900-hp Winton engines. Standardization of parts and modules was already taking place. (BNSF Photo)

One last shot at an articulated train had already been planned months ahead and was about to leave the shop in the form of the new *Twin Cities Zephyrs*. In November 1936, the two trains emerged to be known as the *Morning Zephyr* and the *Afternoon Zephyr*.

These fully articulated six-car trains were, like the Denver trains, framed up in Budd's Pennsylvania plant and then finished in the new 74-acre Electro-Motive plant in McCook, Illinois, near LaGrange. They entered revenue service on December 18, 1936. The 9904 Zephyr was named *Pegasus* and the 9905 *Zephyrus*, with their cars all representing a veritable pantheon of gods – female for *Pegasus* and male for *Zephyrus* – that was grist for the PR department mill.

The locomotives were identical to those hauling the *Denver Zephyrs*,

Gods and Goddesses of the Midwest Rails

Zephyr 9904	Zephyr 9905
Pegasus (loco)	Zephyrus (loco)
Venus (power – cocktail lounge)	Apollo (power – cocktail lounge)
Minerva (coach)	Mars (coach)
Ceres (diner)	Vulcan (diner)
Diana (parlor)	Mercury (diner)
Juno (parlor-observation)	Jupiter (parlor-observation)

mounting two 12-cylinder Winton 201A engines generating 1,800 total horsepower to four GE 716 C 600-volt traction motors, a pair to each power truck. As with the Denver trains, the first car was articulated only in the rear truck, allowing the locomotive to be easily removed by uncoupling the Ohio Brass Tight-lock couplers for maintenance or swapping out with the Denver motive power – which happened often. That first car carried the train's power generators, steam heat, crew quarters, and the revenue-generating cocktail lounge.

After the two coach cars, what made the six-car twins interesting were the fourth, fifth, and sixth cars. The fourth car carried the dining concept to its most efficient, combining a full kitchen with the dining room and a telephone to alert passengers in the cocktail lounge that their table was ready. The fifth was a parlor car featuring rotating upholstered lounge chairs for viewing scenery or making conversation. At the car's rear was a private drawing room with no berth, but a private lavatory and a pair of transverse couches. The rotating parlor chairs continued in the last car, ending with only six armchairs in the observation space.

Heaping on the amenities, designers placed reclining double seats in passenger sections that also allowed tables to be set up between facing pairs. Card-playing areas were designated. Phonographs were installed to supplement the radio,

A unique configuration in the Zephyr fleet, the last car of the 9904 Twin Zephyr's consist – named after Juno, the queen of the Greek (and Roman) gods – made use of 24 swiveling armchairs lining the aisle all the way back to the observation lounge. Upholstered in tan and fawn fabric over rubber cushions, the rotating chairs allowed easy conversation with fellow travelers. A card-playing area with a table was also set aside near the rear just ahead of the six armchairs that formed the observation parlor. Behind the photographer, the 75-foot coach offered restrooms and a private drawing room besides more parlor-chair seating. (BNSF Photo)

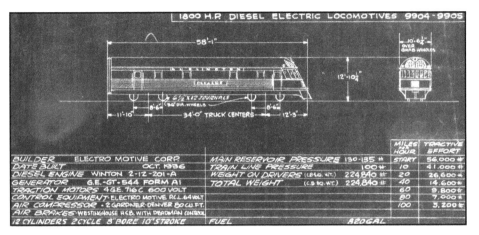

1800 H.P. DIESEL ELECTRIC LOCOMOTIVES 9904-9905

BUILDER	ELECTRO MOTIVE CORP.	MAIN RESERVOIR PRESSURE	130-135 #	MILES PER HOUR	TRACTIVE EFFORT
DATE BUILT	OCT. 1936	TRAIN LINE PRESSURE	100 #	START	56,000 #
DIESEL ENGINE	WINTON 2-12-201-A	WEIGHT ON DRIVERS (B&G. WT.)	224,840 #	10	41,000 #
GENERATOR	G.E.-GT-544 FORM A1	TOTAL WEIGHT (C.B. EQ. WT.)	224,840 #	20	26,600 #
TRACTION MOTORS	4 G.E. 716C 600 VOLT			40	14,600 #
CONTROL EQUIPMENT	ELECTRO MOTIVE P.C.L. 64 VOLT			60	9,800 #
AIR COMPRESSOR	2 GARDNER-DENVER 80 CU.FT.			80	7,000 #
AIR BRAKES	WESTINGHOUSE H6B WITH DEADMAN CONTROL			100	5,200 #
12 CYLINDERS 2CYCLE 8"BORE 10"STROKE		FUEL	420 GAL		

While the Twin Zephyr Pegasus resembles the others of her line, this blueprint notes one important difference. We are shown one 58-foot power car and not an articulated connection to the next car. Pegasus and its twin, Zephyrus, were independent locomotives connected to their rest of the train with Ohio Brass Tight-lock couplers. The second car behind Pegasus, Venus, carried train power, a small baggage compartment, and a cocktail lounge, and was independent in the front and articulated in the rear. (Burlington Route Historical Society)

Sweeping around a bend in the Mississippi is one of the new Twin Zephyrs that became known as the Afternoon Zephyr. The other Twin had become the Morning Zephyr. These eight-car streamlined trains were always booked ahead and most times ran at capacity of 120 passengers, offering a dining room with meals, cocktails, piped-in recorded music or radio shows, and the most beautiful scenery along Old Man River. (Jim Singer Collection)

With delivery of the new Twin Zephyrs 9904 and 9905 lagging, the Burlington leased this General Electric box cab No. 511 from the Electro-Motive Corp. in September 1936 to stand in for the Zephyrs, one or both, until they were ready. To create the illusion of modernity, the Burlington boys slopped on a coat of silver paint and shoved the old hen out the shop door. The 511 and her sister 512 hung around until everything straightened out and then went home, to be scrapped, in 1938. She's shown here hauling heavyweight varnish past the ever-present Otto Perry. (Denver Public Library, Otto Perry Photograph)

Otto Perry either dodged the yard bulls, or they knew him on sight by now, to photograph the Morning Zephyr driving west out of Chicago to turn north for its long ride to Minneapolis on August 11, 1939. This train runs seven cars behind the 9905 Zephyrus power car followed by Apollo, its engine power-baggage-cocktail lounge car. The Chicago Post Office looms in the background as the driver notches up the throttle and the fireman begins to slide shut the front window normally left open at slow yard speeds. (Denver Public Library, Otto Perry Collection)

With the new multi-car Twin Zephyrs in place toward the end of 1936, the original three-car 9901 and 9902 were released for duty elsewhere. The 9901 headed west to Texas and became the Sam Houston Zephyr, while the 9902 went to work in Missouri on the new Ozark State Zephyr service, becoming the Alton Burlington on its nose panel. In 1938 the 9902 was bought by the Burlington-Rock Island and ended up as the Sam Houston Zephyr, while the original SH became the Texas Rocket. Still later, the 9903 and the 9908 also carried the "Alton Burlington" nose art in revenue service. (Burlington Route Historical Society)

but eventually gave way to prerecorded wire programming without a skipping needle. The trains were hugely popular and profitable.

To ring down the curtain on the articulated Zephyr concept, the Burlington asked Budd to produce a four-car train that became their bridge between the now-outdated shovelnose design and the new Electro-Motive E model ("E" stands for "Eighteen hundred horsepower") covered wagons. The new E models were in construction and beginning to see service with other railroads when the *General Pershing Zephyr* rolled out the shop door. The motive power was, essentially, a baggage car named the *Silver Charger* with an engine and shovelnose cab attached.

Later hauled by an EMD E-5 or F road diesel, this collection of Twin Cities Zephyr *dome cars is hauled across the James Hill Bridge in the mid-1940s. The train carried no sleeper but offered a diner car, parlor car, and the first "vista domes" to watch Mississippi River scenery roll past. Note the Twin shovelnose is backed up with an EMD B unit blowing exhaust from (most likely) a ubiquitous EMD 567 two-cycle diesel engine that replaced the aging Wintons. (Jim Singer Collection)*

Gussied up with an artist's airbrush, the 9905 Zephyrus Twin Cities Zephyr poses with seven cars trailing behind for an unknown public-relations flack's photographer. (Jim Singer Collection)

CHAPTER NINE

THE *GENERAL PERSHING* ZEPHYR 9908

Compared to the previous Zephyrs, the 9908 Silver Charger had a brutish, big-shoul-dered look to it, which looked somewhat odd tagged onto the head end of its three-car General Pershing train. With that oversize, six-wheel Blomberg front truck clawing it along, the 9908 looks like it could pull a half-mile of varnish. The big dual horns peering over the headlight have a get-out-of-my way arrogance. The roof is also fluted instead of smooth stainless as with the Denver locos. (Burlington Route Historical Society)

Designed on the boards as a non-articulated train with individual coaches, the *General Pershing* incorporated everything Budd and the Burlington had learned throughout the cycle of Zephyrs. From the more spacious cab with seats for three crewmen to the Electro-Motive 567 diesel engine rated 1,000 hp at their backs, the 78-foot unit was no longer an integral part of the train, but was now a true locomotive capable of hauling any consist, a feature that would extend its service life.

Most conspicuous was the six-wheel "A1A" power truck that went on to be a standard design for Electro-

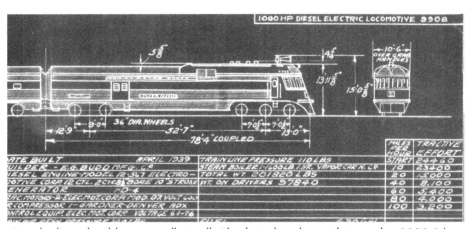

One look at this blueprint tells it all. The last shovelnose design, the 9908 Silver Charger, was a Budd shell over an Electro-Motive design just waiting to become an E model. Under the hood, the grand old Winton had been replaced by a 12-cylinder Electro-Motive Corporation 567 that would go on to become the industry standard. The biggest difference was the huge Blomberg six-wheel front truck replacing the four-wheel design. (Burlington Route Historical Society)

Drumheads were fastened to brass and iron railings that fenced in the open rear deck of the observation car. When heavyweight varnish ruled, the passenger routes were often elaborate and, later on, illuminated with electric light. Round like a drum, they became signatures of the legendary passenger trains that wore them. The Zephyrs' somewhat limited backsides required a more subtle approach. Here, John J. Pershing's signature, incised in stainless steel and flanked by the four stars of his general rank, serves as the 9908 General Pershing drumhead. (Burlington Route Historical Society)

Motive's later models. Designed by Electro-Motive's engineer, Martin Blomberg, the truck was huge with a 14-foot, six-inch wheelbase running 36-inch wheels on two axles powered by a pair of Electro-Motive traction motors with the center axle rolling as an idler and to help with weight distribution. The Blomberg truck's biggest asset was its smooth operation at high speed. The Zephyrs and all other high-speed "motors" tend to rock and roll from side to side, which causes sway and results in worn track and wheel sets. This "nosing" or "hunting" did not plague articulated trains as badly, but the *General Pershing Zephyr* broke that mold and Blomberg's fully equalized – longitudinal, lateral, vertical, pitch, yaw, and roll compensation – swing-bolster design minimized the problem and allowed smooth tracking through curves regardless of speed.

When it came to stopping this hurtling mass, the *General Pershing Zephyr* offered yet another innovation. The four-wheel passenger trucks hold-

ing up its four coaches came equipped with the first disc brakes.

Powering this locomotive was the 567 diesel that would become the most ubiquitous power plant in the Electro-Motive diesel fleet. This V-12 engine replaced the latest version of the Winton 201A that produced 900 hp at 750 rpm. Adding a half-inch to the bore diameter and 50 rpm produced 100 more horsepower.

Perhaps most important, Electro-Motive had developed the 567 as a successor to the Winton 201A diesel engine, and first used the new power plant in Seaboard E4 passenger locomotives of 1938. Between the two engines, the power differential was considerable. Where the 201A's cylinders had a bore of 8 inches and a stroke of 10 inches, producing 900 hp at 750 rpm in the 12-cylinder version, the 567 featured 8-1/2 x 10-inch cylinders each with a displacement of 567 cubic inches, accounting for the model designation and cranked out 1,000 hp at a slightly faster 800 rpm in the V-12 variant.

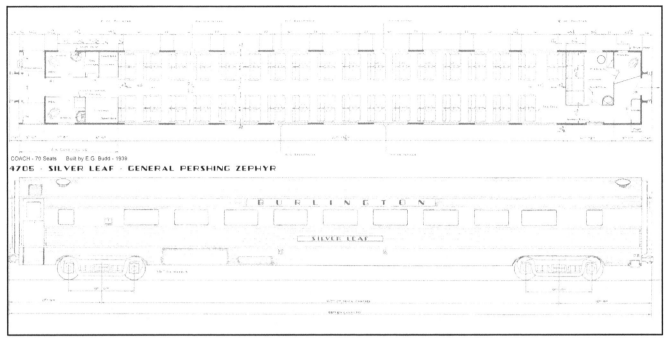

As the Zephyrs matured, their designs began to resemble the new lightweight passenger cars and motive power that followed in the wake of their revolution. The 9908 General Pershing train of 1938 was the last to be hauled by a shovel-nose-style locomotive. The cars, however, would continue service with other trains because the joys of standardization had arrived. This Budd floor plan for the 70-seat Silver Leaf coach is typical of and interchangeable with coaches running on other railroads. (Courtesy, Railway Age)

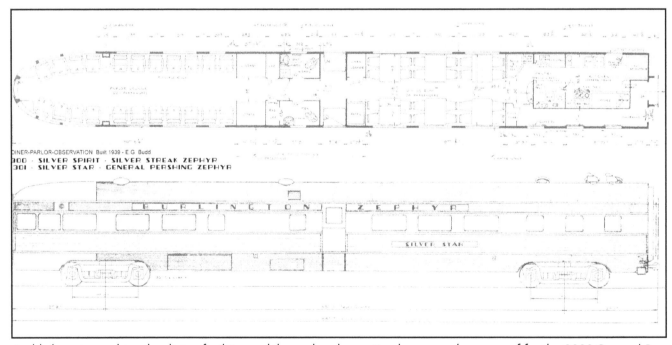

Budd chose to combine the dining facilities and the parlor-observation lounge under one roof for the 9908 General Pershing's 1939 season in the No. 300 Silver Star (which was numbered 300 on the Silver Streak Zephyr). A complete kitchen and 24-passenger dining room made up the front half of the car with the 22-seat parlor-observation car in the rear. This configuration hung a lot of weight on the rear of the train, but the convenience for passengers was obvious. (Courtesy, Railway Age)

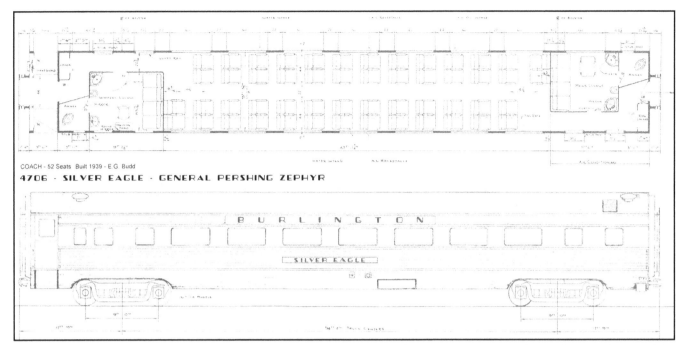

COACH - 52 Seats Built 1939 - E.G. Budd
4706 · SILVER EAGLE · GENERAL PERSHING ZEPHYR

The Silver Eagle *coach for the 9800 offered 52 seats and large men's and women's lounges at either end. It complemented the* Silver Leaf *coach as part of the* General Pershing *three-car train, a throwback to the original* Pioneer/Twins *design. All cars were independent since by 1939, articulation was no longer seen to be either practical or desirable. (Courtesy,* Railway Age)

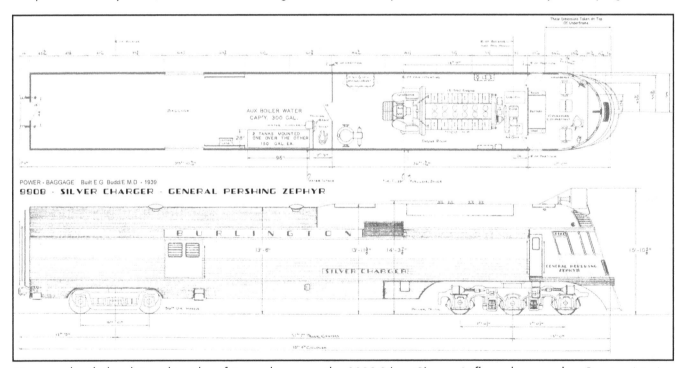

POWER - BAGGAGE Built E.G. Budd/E.M.D - 1939
9908 · SILVER CHARGER · GENERAL PERSHING ZEPHYR

Compared with the cluttered insides of its predecessors, the 9908 Silver Charger's *floor plan reveals a Spartan interior. The cab seems as roomy as the pilot house of a ship with the big EMC 567 12-cylinder engine shoved back behind a partition along with the air compressor. No banging motor and howling generator at the engineer's back. The rest is baggage and an auxiliary boiler – definitely a military man's layout. (Courtesy* Railway Age)

The Zephyrs' fuel and water tanks were slung underneath the body frame for easy access and draining as needed. Diesel service facilities were slow to come until the other railroads began ordering the new high-performance engines. This fuel tank also has a capacity gauge next to its filler plug. (Gerry Souter Photo)

Having the 40-foot open space of the baggage car behind the crew cab allowed the engine to be moved farther back so the generator didn't intrude into the compartment and running noise became less of a fatigue factor. Another beneficiary of this open area was the steam generator for heating passenger spaces. It now resided comfortably in the power car with the other machinery.

The *General Pershing Zephyr* had an elegantly brutish look to it when it went into service over the 558 miles between Kansas City and St. Louis on April 20, 1939. Its name was painted in red on the sides of the power car beneath the cab windows while a stainless plaque proclaimed *Silver Charger*, named after Pershing's horse, midway down the car's flanks. For a five-hour commuter run, this truly was a premium service for its 122 passengers.

Immediately behind the power car/baggage unit rode a chair car, the *Silver Leaf*, for 70 passengers. The women had their own lounge at the head end while men used two toilet facilities flank-

Running at the same time as the 9908 Silver Charger, the 2-10-0 steamer graphically demonstrates the jump in aerodynamic technology between the steam era and the streamlined diesel era ushered in by the Burlington Zephyrs. Every steam locomotive ever built had the same basic components as the earliest steamers built back in the 1820s — only updated and made more efficient. The Zephyrs were new technology from the wheels up. (Gerry Souter Photo)

Here is the full three-car General Pershing train that ran between Kansas City and St. Louis in 1939, a five-hour trip, carrying 122 passengers. This was strictly a daylight run, but offered comfort, food, and a speedy trip. From the Spartan locomotive and baggage section through two well-appointed coaches to the dining room and parlor observation space, the General Pershing took the Pioneer Zephyr's three-car concept to its ultimate realization in just five years. (Courtesy, Railway Age)

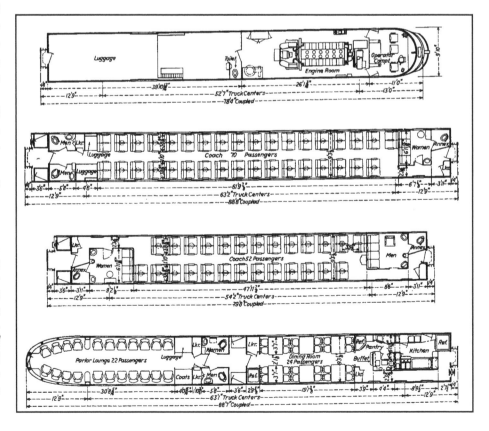

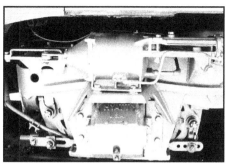

Later in its revenue service, the General Pershing train pauses in the evening at W. Quincy, Illinois. The date is unknown, but the dents in its shovelnose and the rotating Mars light fastened above its standard headlight put the Silver Charger into the second decade of its productive life. (Jim Neubauer Collection)

Typical of the 9908 Silver Charger's entire concept, this is a close-up look at the brake cylinder bolted onto the side of the huge Blomberg power truck. The big EMD truck had been specially designed to eliminate "hunting" the side-to-side movement of wheels on an unevenly gauged track. Everything seemed massive for moving three cars between Kansas City and St. Louis, but the 9908 had a long afterlife when its glory days as a hauler of prime streamlined coaches was over. (Gerry Souter Photo)

In its later life, the Silver Charger lost its General Pershing train and lettering and spent time shuttling around the Burlington system. The great views these windows once offered also damned the concept for safety reasons. As the few wrecks demonstrated, crewmen didn't stand much of a chance in a head-on confrontation. (Gerry Souter Photo)

Now on display at the St. Louis Museum of Transportation, the Silver Charger is still impressive, especially when surrounded by steam engines of its period. Its massive lines are still apparent even with the fluted under-skirting removed, as often happened when efficient maintenance took precedence over design subtleties. (Gerry Souter Photo)

ing the hall at the other end, sharing the space with hand-luggage racks. Following that car was the chair coach *Silver Eagle* for 52 passengers. It came complete with a full men's lounge and a second women's lounge facility before passing through the vestibule and by a 13-foot kitchen and buffet area. The kitchen and wait staff served a fully fitted-out 19-foot dining room that seated 24 patrons for full-course meals or snacks.

Refreshed, the traveler with cash enough to support a parlor lounge reservation at the rear of the train returned to his or her chair in line with the other patrons. This 31-foot section offered 22 passengers their own coat and luggage

The rotating Mars light mounted on the 9908 became a safety addition on all the Zephyrs and most other locomotives in the 1950s. Fatal road-crossing accidents increased where auto traffic had mushroomed, but building effective gate and light warning systems had not kept pace. (Gerry Souter Photo)

Even in retirement, the 9908 Silver Charger *projects a massive arrogance that made heads turn in its prime. The volunteers at the Museum of Transportation still climb inside every few months, crank over the big 567 diesel engine, and let it idle for a while. Without too much work, they claim, the 9908 could shoulder its way back out onto the main. (Gerry Souter Photo)*

Resting on its display track at the St. Louis Museum of Transportation, the 9908 Silver Charger *remains impressive even in repose. The big shovelnose rests on that huge A1A Blomberg power truck that was the model for future power trucks on E-, F-, and FT-model diesel locomotives. The concept ended with the 9908 as the final test bed for the next generation of famous Zephyr trains. (Gerry Souter Photo)*

The standard four-wheel truck was still used with the huge Blomberg six-wheeler on the 9908, but the distance between wheel centers was increased to nine feet from the eight-foot, six-inch trucks used on the 9906 and 9907. The wheel size had also increased from a 30- to a 36-inch diameter. (Gerry Souter Photo)

Timken bearings, as shown on this close-up of the four-wheel truck beneath the 9908 Silver Charger, had become the railroad standard. Six-inch Timken bearings had been standard equipment on the original Pioneer Zephyr back in 1934 and stayed with the fleet. As the power increased, the wheel size also increased from 30 to 36 inches. (Gerry Souter Photo)

When the 9908 made its station stops, the batteries, which stored power created by the generators, were supplemented by electrical input through this plug receptor beneath the frame. Wherever the train was parked for a period of time with systems in operation, auxiliary power was required. (Gerry Souter Photo)

racks, toilet facilities, and a sweeping panorama of the passing countryside. Enunciator buttons summoned waiters for beverage service. Lighting came from recessed fixtures above the chairs. In the coaches, overall fluorescent lighting provided more than adequate reading levels – yet another innovation. And, of course, as with the other *Zephyrs*, the interior was sealed with safety-glass windows and cooled with air conditioning.

While the first *Pioneer Zephyr* mixed colors favoring blues, pearls, and grays, the *General Pershing's* designers chose a more rustic and manly blend of tans, sandstones, browns, and rusts for its walls, LinoTile floors, Chase Seamloc carpets, draperies, and fixtures. Again, Paul Cret was the design house for this one-of-a-kind train. From first to the last Zephyr, the parlor lounge also offered more comfortable parlor chairs and eliminated the writing desk at the very end of the room in favor of a bolted rear exit door. On the other side of that exit was the so-called signature "drumhead," traditionally familiar on observation-car open vestibules. On the 9908's streamlined stern, this touch translated into a reproduction of John "Black Jack" Pershing's signature etched in stainless steel.

EMC engineer Martin Blomberg designed the immense swing-bolster six-wheel power truck. The six 36-inch wheels were housed in a 14-foot wheelbase that was created to improve locomotive performance at high speed on uneven track. Until then, all high-speed locomotives experienced "hunting" of the flanged wheels on the rail surface. Along with pitch, yaw, and roll compensation, this annoying and wear-causing problem was addressed in the truck. The Blomberg truck went on to become a standard on diesel locomotives. The 9908 acted as a test bed that proved the concept. Note the brake cylinders on the front and rear axles while the center axle is an idler with the speedometer attached. (Gerry Souter Photo)

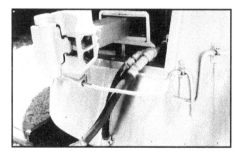

Another compensation for old age, the 9908 had a front coupler permanently mounted in its shiny shovelnose. This modification was added to virtually all shovelnoses that survived into general service hauling before the scrap yard or display duty called. No longer the kings and queens of the high iron, they had to earn their keep at any job that came to hand. (Gerry Souter Photo)

CHAPTER TEN

CONCLUSION

The Pioneer Zephyr shines again after 20 years of service. In 1960, the Zephyr was retired and, instead of ending up in the scrap yard, was sent to the Museum of Science and Industry in Chicago as a display in the museum's front yard. Here, mimicking the unveiling of the Zephyr in 1934 by CB&Q employees, workers at the Northern Rail Car shop haul the polished streamliner back into the sunlight. (Jim Neubauer Collection)

With the *General Pershing* filling out the last of the shovelnose fleet, the railroads sailed into World War II and helped win a war fought from both coasts. That emergency grind wore down all the roads and, except for 9901, which was burned beyond repair in a 1944 fire, in the 1950s the amazing silver streaks that once blistered tracks and fired imaginations fell to the scrapper's torch or retired. The first Zephyr, the 9900 *Pioneer*, outlasted the rest and retired in 1960. The restored streamliner rests at Chicago's Museum of Science and Industry while the last, the 9908 *Silver Charger*, is displayed at the St. Louis Museum of Transportation. The only non-Burlington shovelnose, the *Flying Yankee*, is undergoing full restoration in Claremont, New Hampshire. If the restorers are successful, maybe another generation can know what it's like to stand on a hillside and hear that sound and see that flash of silver and know something exciting, something they've never seen before, is rushing down the track.

The polished front end of the 9900 Pioneer Zephyr looks back at visitors to Chicago's Museum of Science and Industry. To the left is the end of a ramp that runs most of the train's length at station platform height. The entire exhibit is a paean to Art Deco design in 20th-century technology with the Zephyr as its centerpiece. Both the interior and exterior have been restored to their appearance in about 1935, though the story told by guides is the 1934 record-breaking run. A well-done AV show runs from the mail room to the parlor lounge. (Scott Brownell photo, courtesy, Museum of Science and Industry, Chicago)

Condensed
Train Schedules

Even with the new E- and F-model diesels coming from the Electro-Motive Division of General Motors, the shovelnoses hung on as a valued revenue generator, as attested to by this 1947 schedule. The big "covered wagon" diesels would dominate as steam slipped away by the 1960s and the silver streak Zephyrs were picked off as they wore out. Now that their work is finished, the remaining few are reminders of an amazing era when a nation needed success stories. (Courtesy, Flying Yankee Restoration Group)

On January 4, 1944, while operating between McCook, Illinois, and Lincoln, Nebraska, the four-car Pioneer Zephyr parked next to one of the Burlington's "next generation" diesels from Electro-Motive, an FT (Freight–Twenty-seven hundred horsepower) "covered wagon." The more crew-friendly design of the early E, F, and FT locomotives that followed set the design pattern for the next 40 years. (Fred Lehmann Photo, Jim Singer Collection)

LEFT: Twenty years of rail service takes a lot out of a train designed to operate in one piece. When the Pioneer Zephyr retired in 1960, the well-worn exterior was in need of freshening up. Before being shipped to its final resting place, the restorers at Northern Railcar gave the Zephyr's stainless exterior a spit-shine. The interior did not require work since the public did not enter the display. (Jim Neubauer Collection)

Rolling through winter snow, the Pioneer Zephyr makes its final run toward retirement at Chicago's Museum of Science and Industry in 1960. Outlived by less stylish E- and F-model diesel workhorses, the old record-breaking shovelnose still turned heads in its last years. (Jim Neubauer Collection)

BELOW: Still gleaming in the morning sun, the stainless-steel Pioneer Zephyr steams at a station platform in 1960, the year of its retirement. Railroads were loading up with diesel locomotives as fast as they could scrap their old steamers, and it was this three-car wonder that showed the way. (Jim Neubauer Collection)

All tricked out with new safety lamps and buttoned up against the Midwestern cold, the Pioneer quietly idles as its last days slip away in 1960. (Jim Neubauer Collection)

Burlington Route

Stretched out full-length, the Pioneer Zephyr rests next to the World War II German U-boat, U-505, on what was supposed to be permanent exhibit Chicago's Museum of Science and Industry. It suffered in the elements over the years and became a home to many stray cats. Eventually, Museum expansion required both these exhibits to be moved, and the Pioneer was packed off to a restoration shop. (Jim Singer Collection)

Sun sets on the 9900 Pioneer Zephyr as it rests in Galesburg, Illinois, on its way to permanent retirement in 1960. Passengers climb aboard for one last ride on the train that changed the railroads. (Jim Neubauer Collection)

Oil streaks down the stainless-steel shovel-nose at Chicago's Museum of Science and Industry. The retired Pioneer Zephyr moldered away on its exhibition track for 40 years with touch-ups only here and there. It achieved eyesore status before being lovingly restored and moved inside the museum, an Art Deco relic of a time when passenger trains ruled the rails. (Burlington Route Historical Society Collection)

The 9900 Pioneer *Zephyr stands on a stub end of track next to the German U-boat, U-505, as part of an outdoor display at Chicago's Museum of Science and Industry. After being pulled from service, the 9900 was fortunate to be restored to its original exterior appearance in 1960. Eventually, the Zephyr lost pride of place and was shuffled around to the side of the building. But, once again, it was saved from the scrap yard and now resides inside the building in a showplace all its own, almost fully restored inside and out. (BNSF Photo)*

Model Makers Keep Zephyrs Alive

Though the full-size Zephyrs have been scrapped or mothballed and the *Flying Yankee* moves toward restoration one contribution at a time, the silver trains can still be seen tearing down the tracks. On model layouts across the country, both O-Gauge and HO-Gauge versions of the Zephyr clatter across switch points and around banked turns at scale speed.

Mike's Train Shop (MTS), the most prolific producer of high-quality scale and almost-scale O-Gauge and Hi-rail trains, has twice pushed versions of the *Pioneer Zephyr* out the shop door. They run on three-rail tracks and, while they are not exact copies, they embody the spirit of Budd's concept and give their engine drivers a feel for the 1930s Art Deco appeal of these unique designs.

Railway Classics brought out an HO-Gauge model of the *Twin Cities Zephyr* in exquisite brass. Though half the size of the O-Gauge versions, this scale model is an exact replica of the 1936 *Twin* with extra capacity. It represents the latest in modern technology to create a head-turning result.

This model from MTS faithfully captures the early-era Pioneer Zephyr with the original headlight, but the scale look is slightly squashed to get around tighter tin-plate O-gauge turns. (Courtesy, MTS Electric Trains, Inc.)

Released by MTS (Mike's Train Shop) in semi-scale O-Gauge, this model gets the job done on three-rail track still needing large radius turns. Its era is later than the Pioneer or the first Twins' debut. The Mars light atop takes it into the late 1940s, early 1950s. Its look is more "Cyborg Zephyr" assembled from pieces. (Courtesy, MTS Electric Trains, Inc.)

This model in HO scale is a faithful reproduction of Zephyrus, one of the new Twin Cities Zephyrs. This seven-car beauty is cast in brass for the discerning modeler with deep pockets. Built in limited quantities, the details are exquisite. Many modelers subscribe for the trains before they are issued. Their collector's value is considerable if you never take it out of the box. New can motors and computer-chip controls, however, make operating these brass beauties a pleasure. (Courtesy, Ken Patterson, Railway Classics)

Books/Magazine Articles

The Early Zephyrs, Geoffrey H. Doughty, TLC Publishing, Lynchburg, Virginia, 2002

The Burlington Route, Richard C. Overton, Alfred A. Knopf, New York, 1965

Diesels West! The Evolution of Power on the Burlington, David P. Morgan, Kalmbach Publishing, Milwaukee, Wisconsin, 1963

The Pioneer Zephyr, R. W. Rediske, 1st Books, Bloomington, Indiana, 2002

Railway Age, NYC, April 14, 1934, "Burlington Zephyr Completed at Budd Plant," Ralph Budd

The Traffic World, April 14, 1934, "The Burlington Zephyr," Ralph Budd

Endnotes

1. Morgan, David P., *Diesels West!*, Chicago, Burlington & Quincy Railroad Company, Kalmbach Publishing Co., Milwaukee, 1963

2. Chicago, Burlington & Quincy Railroad, "Burlington Zephyr Completed at Budd Plant," *Railway Age Magazine*, April 14, 1934, NYC

3. Wagner, Hol, "Shovelnoses," *Burlington Bulletin*, Burlington Road Historical Society, 4th Quarter, 1984

4. Ibid, Wagner, Hol, "Shovelnoses," *Burlington Bulletin*

5. Yard Limit Spotters Guide, History of EMD diesel engines, http://yardlimit.railfan.net/emd/

6. Budd, Ralph, "The Burlington Zephyr," *The Traffic World Magazine*, April 14, 1934, pg. 710

7. Ibid, Wagner, Hol, "Shovelnoses," *Burlington Bulletin*

8. Ibid, "Burlington Zephyr Completed at Budd Plant," *Railway Age Magazine*, pg. 17

9. *Greenberg's Guide to American Flyer O Gauge*, Steven H. Kimball (editor), Simon Chaplin, Greenberg Publishing Company, Sykesville, MD 1987

10. *Greenberg's Guide to American Flyer O Gauge*, Steven H. Kimball (editor), Simon Chaplin, Greenberg Publishing Company, Sykesville, MD 1987

11. Rediske, 000R.W. *The Pioneer Zephyr*, 1st Books Library, Bloomington, Indiana, 2000

12. Burlington Archives, *CB&Q Division Operations Memoranda*, March 6, 1939, Segment quoted. Courtesy, Newberry Library, Chicago, Illinois

Model Makers Keep Zephyrs Alive

Though the full-size Zephyrs have been scrapped or mothballed and the *Flying Yankee* moves toward restoration one contribution at a time, the silver trains can still be seen tearing down the tracks. On model layouts across the country, both O-Gauge and HO-Gauge versions of the Zephyr clatter across switch points and around banked turns at scale speed.

Mike's Train Shop (MTS), the most prolific producer of high-quality scale and almost-scale O-Gauge and Hi-rail trains, has twice pushed versions of the *Pioneer Zephyr* out the shop door. They run on three-rail tracks and, while they are not exact copies, they embody the spirit of Budd's concept and give their engine drivers a feel for the 1930s Art Deco appeal of these unique designs.

Railway Classics brought out an HO-Gauge model of the *Twin Cities Zephyr* in exquisite brass. Though half the size of the O-Gauge versions, this scale model is an exact replica of the 1936 *Twin* with extra capacity. It represents the latest in modern technology to create a head-turning result.

This model from MTS faithfully captures the early-era Pioneer Zephyr *with the original headlight, but the scale look is slightly squashed to get around tighter tin-plate O-gauge turns. (Courtesy, MTS Electric Trains, Inc.)*

Released by MTS (Mike's Train Shop) in semi-scale O-Gauge, this model gets the job done on three-rail track still needing large radius turns. Its era is later than the Pioneer or the first Twins' *debut. The Mars light atop takes it into the late 1940s, early 1950s. Its look is more "Cyborg Zephyr" assembled from pieces. (Courtesy, MTS Electric Trains, Inc.)*

This model in HO scale is a faithful reproduction of Zephyrus, one of the new Twin Cities Zephyrs. *This seven-car beauty is cast in brass for the discerning modeler with deep pockets. Built in limited quantities, the details are exquisite. Many modelers subscribe for the trains before they are issued. Their collector's value is considerable if you never take it out of the box. New can motors and computer-chip controls, however, make operating these brass beauties a pleasure. (Courtesy, Ken Patterson, Railway Classics)*

Books/Magazine Articles

The Early Zephyrs, Geoffrey H. Doughty, TLC Publishing, Lynchburg, Virginia, 2002

The Burlington Route, Richard C. Overton, Alfred A. Knopf, New York, 1965

Diesels West! The Evolution of Power on the Burlington, David P. Morgan, Kalmbach Publishing, Milwaukee, Wisconsin, 1963

The Pioneer Zephyr, R. W. Rediske, 1st Books, Bloomington, Indiana, 2002

Railway Age, NYC, April 14, 1934, "Burlington Zephyr Completed at Budd Plant," Ralph Budd

The Traffic World, April 14, 1934, "The Burlington Zephyr," Ralph Budd

Endnotes

1. Morgan, David P., *Diesels West!*, Chicago, Burlington & Quincy Railroad Company, Kalmbach Publishing Co., Milwaukee, 1963

2. Chicago, Burlington & Quincy Railroad, "Burlington Zephyr Completed at Budd Plant," *Railway Age Magazine*, April 14, 1934, NYC

3. Wagner, Hol, "Shovelnoses," *Burlington Bulletin*, Burlington Road Historical Society, 4th Quarter, 1984

4. Ibid, Wagner, Hol, "Shovelnoses," *Burlington Bulletin*

5. Yard Limit Spotters Guide, History of EMD diesel engines, http://yardlimit.railfan.net/emd/

6. Budd, Ralph, "The Burlington Zephyr," *The Traffic World Magazine*, April 14, 1934, pg. 710

7. Ibid, Wagner, Hol, "Shovelnoses," *Burlington Bulletin*

8. Ibid, "Burlington Zephyr Completed at Budd Plant," *Railway Age Magazine*, pg. 17

9. *Greenberg's Guide to American Flyer O Gauge*, Steven H. Kimball (editor), Simon Chaplin, Greenberg Publishing Company, Sykesville, MD 1987

10. *Greenberg's Guide to American Flyer O Gauge*, Steven H. Kimball (editor), Simon Chaplin, Greenberg Publishing Company, Sykesville, MD 1987

11. Rediske, 000R.W. *The Pioneer Zephyr*, 1st Books Library, Bloomington, Indiana, 2000

12. Burlington Archives, *CB&Q Division Operations Memoranda*, March 6, 1939, Segment quoted. Courtesy, Newberry Library, Chicago, Illinois

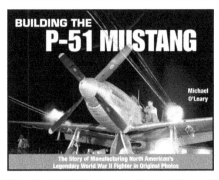
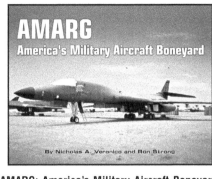
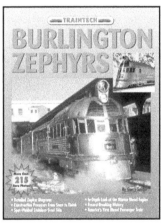

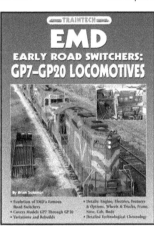
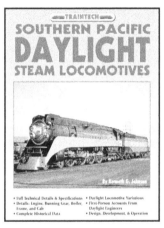

9 781580 071918